ECONOMIC AND SOCIAL COMMISSION FOR ASIA AND THE PACIFIC

PRODUCTION AND DISTRIBUTION OF ASSISTIVE DEVICES FOR PEOPLE WITH DISABILITIES

PART ONE:
REGIONAL REVIEW

UNITED NATIONS
New York, 1997

ST/ESCAP/1774

UNITED NATIONS PUBLICATION
Sales No. E.98.II.F.7
Copyright © United Nations 1997
ISBN: 92-1-119775-9

PREFACE

Full participation and equality is the goal of the Asian and Pacific Decade of Disabled Persons, 1993-2002. Achievement of this goal involves creating an environment that welcomes the inclusion of persons with disabilities in mainstream community life.

With respect to the reduction of the physical barriers to inclusion, there are two essential and complementary means. One is through the creation of barrier-free built environments. The other is through increasing the availability of appropriate assistive devices, with the requisite services for needs assessment, training, follow-up, as well as repair and maintenance.

ESCAP's on-going work on the promotion of non-handicapping environments for persons with disabilities and older persons in the Asia-Pacific region, including accessible public transport systems and services, seeks to enhance the first means. The present publication is the outcome of ESCAP's initial efforts to strengthen the second means.

In the developing countries of the ESCAP region, relatively few people have the use of assistive devices which are essential for freedom of movement and choice in daily life. Those who do are likely to be found in large urban centres, where rehabilitation services are concentrated. Among them are those who can afford to buy the most expensive services and devices available on the market. This publication is not about assistive devices for the privileged few. Instead, the focus is on the needs of the majority who are excluded from services and opportunities.

This publication is part of an ESCAP project entitled "Promotion of regional cooperation for the local production of assistive devices for persons with disabilities". The project grew out of serious concern over the limited availability of culturally-appropriate, high-quality and low-cost assistive devices. At the same time, it was recognized that the potential existed within the region for addressing this concern.

The exchanges and information dissemination under the project are a contribution to technical cooperation, especially among developing countries, to spur greater effort on assistive devices for the poor. This publication is primarily aimed at senior policy makers and programme personnel in diverse mainstream development sectors.

Established channels will direct an ESCAP publication concerning disabled persons to departments for social welfare and community development. The issues raised in this publication, however, require the attention of senior personnel responsible for national development planning, science and technology education, research and development, manufacture of industrial materials, poverty alleviation, rural development, primary health care, skills development, employment promotion, as well as coordination of non-governmental organizations, development aid and technical cooperation.

The publication demystifies the subject so that the above-mentioned senior personnel can use their positions to support improvements in local innovation, production and distribution of assistive devices. They can achieve this through policy decisions and resource allocations. By raising issues concerning the subject of appropriate assistive devices in the forums they participate in, senior personnel can include it in the development agenda. The recommendations and sample national plan in Part I of the publication are a guide to action by this group. In this way, senior policy makers and programme personnel can be part of a wider endeavour to help harness the potential within the ESCAP region, to benefit millions of disabled persons.

The seed for the project was planted by Mr. Rafeeudin Ahmed, who was Executive Secretary of ESCAP from April 1992, when the Commission declared the Decade, until September 1994, when he assumed the position of Associate Administrator of UNDP. Subsequent development and implementation of the project was further inspired by pioneers in the field, both individuals and organizations, whose work is cited in the publication.

The publication is based on a manuscript prepared by Mr. R. Saha, Director, Department of Science and Technology, Government of India, in his capacity as consultant to ESCAP. Among the challenges faced by the Secretariat in undertaking this new work was the difficulty of obtaining comprehensive information. The difficulty was compounded by the fact that, in many cases, current information was not documented at all or was not available in English. Thus, with this publication, it is hoped that many more will be encouraged to join in regional networking, to enrich the indigenous production of assistive devices.

The Government of the Republic of Korea extended generous funding support for the project. That funding support enabled the Secretariat to take the first step towards helping to meet the region's critical need for information dissemination and networking on indigenous assistive devices.

The Government of India contributed additional funding and technical support, particularly through the hosting of the Technical Workshop on the Indigenous Production and Distribution of Assistive Devices, held at Madras (now known as Chennai), India, from 5 to 14 September 1995.

iv

Handicap International's funding support also enhanced participation in the Workshop. For excellent cooperation extended in the finalization of the publication, the Secretariat is grateful to Handicap International (HI) staff at Bangkok (Mr. Yann Drouet and Ms. Maria Carmen-Seage), Phnom Penh (Mr. Marc Bonnet) and Paris (Dr. Philippe Chabasse and Mr. Abdi Bouheddi).

Appreciation is due to all who contributed to the publication; their names are indicated in the relevant sections.

In addition to HI, the Secretariat is grateful to other members of the Subcommittee on Disability-related Concerns of the Regional Interagency Committee for Asia and the Pacific (RICAP), as well as its network partners, who reviewed relevant parts of the manuscript and/or contributed items for inclusion. The following were particularly helpful: Mr. Douglas Krefting of the Centre for Disability in Development (Bangladesh), Ms. Mohua Paul of the Centre for the Rehabilitation of the Paralysed (Bangladesh), Mr. Johann Borg of Inter-Life Bangladesh, Mr. Sun Zhonghua of the China Disabled Persons' Federation, Colonel D.S. Vohra of Nevedac Prosthetic Centre (India), Dr. Nurul Ainy Sidik of the Ministry of Health, Government of Indonesia, Dr. Gerry Heryati of Fatmawati Hospital (Indonesia), Ms. Francesca Ortali, CBR Consultant of the CBR Office, South Sulawesi (Indonesia), Ms. Venus Ilagan of Disabled Peoples' International (DPI)-Philippines, Mr. Lee Sang Yong of the Ministry of Health and Welfare (Republic of Korea), Mr. Cyril Siriwardene of the Sri Lanka Foundation for the Rehabilitation of the Disabled, Colonel Topong Kulkanichit of DPI-Thailand, Ms. Anuradha Mohit of the Asian Blind Union, Mr. William Brohier of Christoffel-Blindenmission, Ms. Tanya Packer of the International Centre for the Advancement of Community Based Rehabilitation (ICACBR), Mr. Tomas Lagerwall of the International Commission on Technology and Accessibility (ICTA) Information Centre/Rehabilitation International, and Dr. Han Tun and Dr. Enrico Pupulin of the World Health Organization (WHO).

Furthermore, the Secretariat would like to acknowledge the valuable contributions of Mr. Antony Samy of WORTH Trust (India), Mr. David Werner of HealthWrights (U.S.A.) and the National Research and Development Centre for Welfare and Health (STAKES), Government of Finland, especially Dr. Vappu Taipale, Ms. Anja Leppo and Mr. Jouko Kokko.

Wearing a below-knee leather and wood prosthesis (see p. xiv).

EXECUTIVE SUMMARY

At its forty-eighth session in 1992, the Economic and Social Commission for Asia and the Pacific (**ESCAP**) declared the period 1993-2002 as the **Asian and Pacific Decade of Disabled Persons**, with the goal of **full participation and equality of people with disabilities**. In the following year, at its forty-ninth session, the Commission adopted the Agenda for Action for the Decade. **Assistive devices** (items, such as **prosthetic limbs** and **hearing aids**, that directly enable people with disabilities to participate in the activities of daily life) constitute an important area of that Agenda. For many people with disabilities in the **developing countries** of the ESCAP region, assistive devices are a **basic need** – a need as important as adequate shelter.

This publication provides information on the indigenous production and distribution of assistive devices in Asian and Pacific developing countries. It has two major **parts**:

1. A **regional review** of production and distribution of assistive devices in Asian and Pacific developing countries;

2. The **proceedings** of the **Technical Workshop** on the Indigenous Production and Distribution of Assistive Devices held in **Madras**,[1] India, in September 1995, including the **papers** presented;

The publication also contains three **supplements**:

(a) A **directory** of assistive-device **producers** located in Asian and Pacific developing countries;

(b) A listing of international and national **mandates** pertaining to assistive devices;

(c) **Technical** specifications and information pertaining to some types of assistive devices of particular relevance for small workshops and organizations concerned with community-based rehabilitation.

The regional review covers issues under the following **headings**:

(a) Measures by which assistive devices enhance **inclusion in society**, when combined with **accessible environments** and social **attitude changes** in the home, work place and wider community;

(b) The **design and production** of **specific devices and their parts**, including choice of proper **materials** and design **styles** to ensure that a device is appropriate for its user;

---

[1] Officially renamed Chennai in 1996.

(c) Strategies for **indigenous production**, including difficulties faced with regard to **import, mass production** and **quality control** of devices and their components;

(d) Methods of **distributing** devices, and **information** about devices, to the **poor** and to the **rural areas** where the need for them is most urgent;

(e) The importance of **repairing and maintaining** devices, especially in the rural areas;

(f) Options for **training** personnel concerned with assistive devices, from **skilled rehabilitation technologists** to **users** themselves;

(g) Approaches to the **innovation** of new devices, from laboratory research to village-level innovation by users;

(h) Areas for **technical cooperation** by which developing countries in the region can help each other improve their services for producing and distributing devices.

A summary of recommendations in the regional review covers **action by** the following **groups:** device designers, producers, health-care personnel, distributors and repair personnel, people with disabilities, and rural development organizations and agencies.

The regional review closes with a sample **national plan** on assistive devices. The plan contains, *inter alia*, the following **recommendations:**

(a) Members of the **United Nations system** could, in close collaboration with Governments and NGOs in the Asia-Pacific region, undertake the following:

    (i) **Share resources** for training and innovation;

    (ii) **Exchange information** on national and local experiences;

    (iii) Facilitate **exchange of devices** within the region;

(b) Governments at the **central** level may take the following actions:

    (i) **Coordinate** assistive-device services within the country;

    (ii) Provide **funding** support;

    (iii) Adopt **appropriate regulations** and procedures;

    (iv) Provide and/or support **services for training**;

(c) Governments at **local**, municipal, regional, provincial or state levels may take the following actions:

    (i) **Collect data** on people with disabilities and assistive devices;

    (ii) Publicize and **distribute information** about assistive devices;

    (iii) **Provide or support services** for the production, distribution, repair and maintenance of assistive devices.

CONTENTS

CONTENTS *(continued)*

CONTENTS *(continued)*

CONTENTS *(continued)*

BOXES

- 15 ปี ต่อมา
- 15 Years later
- 15 Ans après

- คุณสุปัน,
  อรัญประเทศ จังหวัดสระแก้ว ประเทศไทย
- Khun Suphan, Aranyaprathet,
  Sakeaw Province Thailand

Fifteen years later wearing a resin prosthesis.

CHAPTER I

INTRODUCTION

A. Purpose

In the developing countries of Asia and the Pacific, poor people with disabilities are frequently trapped in a vicious cycle of exclusion from society and mainstream development programmes. Without appropriate assistive devices, they often lack the means to participate in education and training programmes for independent living and contribution to the development process. The resulting lack of skills is a barrier to employment. Without income from work, people with disabilities remain poor, and thus unable to purchase assistive devices. Given these conditions, for many people with disabilities, assistive devices are a basic need – a need as important as adequate shelter.

At its forty-eighth session in 1992, the Economic and Social Commission for Asia and the Pacific (ESCAP) declared the period 1993-2002 as the Asian and Pacific Decade of Disabled Persons, with the goal of full participation and equality of people with disabilities. In the following year, at its forty-ninth session, the Commission adopted the Agenda for Action for the Decade. Assistive devices constitute an important area of that Agenda.

Scaling new heights with a prosthesis.

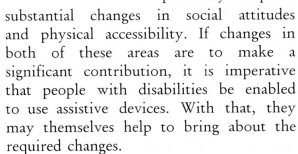

The availability of appropriate assistive devices that are affordable by the majority of people who need them, or by government agencies and non-government organizations (NGOs) working on their behalf, is one of the changes that people with disabilities in Asian and Pacific developing countries require in order to live and work independently. Full equality of opportunity requires substantial changes in social attitudes and physical accessibility. If changes in both of these areas are to make a significant contribution, it is imperative that people with disabilities be enabled to use assistive devices. With that, they may themselves help to bring about the required changes.

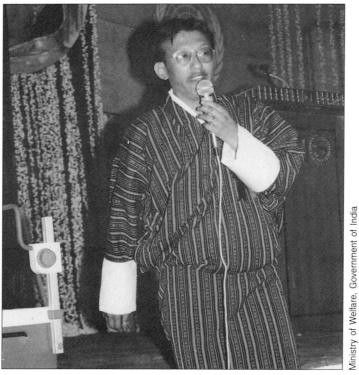

Meeting the need for assistive devices through TCDC.

Following the declaration of the Decade, Governments in the ESCAP region are increasingly interested in introducing and strengthening legislation and policies to protect the rights of people with disabilities. The availability of low-cost, appropriate assistive devices is a necessary part of protecting these rights.

There is a wide gap between the availability of appropriate assistive devices and the need for such devices. Some of the available devices are designed, produced or distributed in such a way that their worth for users is limited. In other cases, the production of new and useful devices is confined to certain geographical areas, while needs elsewhere – within a country or in other parts of the region – remain unmet.

This situation is caused, at least partially, by the inadequate availability of information. So far, personnel working with assistive devices do not have a strong regional network to exchange information. They are often unaware of innovative solutions found elsewhere in the Asia-Pacific region.

The aim of this publication is to help remedy this situation by providing information on the indigenous production and distribution of assistive devices in Asian and Pacific developing

Box 1: Who Can Use This Publication?

This publication is directed at the following groups in the developing countries of the Asia-Pacific region:

(a) Government policy makers and programme personnel responsible for:

(i) Disability issues;

(ii) Health;

(iii) Social welfare and community development;

(iv) Science and technology, especially research and development;

(v) University research;

(vi) Education and training;

(vii) Employment promotion;

(viii) Rural development, especially technology and skill development;

(ix) Technical cooperation among developing countries (TCDC).

(b) University and private research personnel conducting research on:

(i) Disability issues;

(ii) Rural development;

(iii) Technology and applied science.

(c) Management and personnel in industries producing:

(i) Thermoplastics;

(ii) Semiconductors;

(iii) Microcellular rubber;

(iv) Microfibres;

(v) Bicycles;

(vi) Motorcycles.

(d) Personnel of philanthropic organizations supporting:

(i) Equal opportunities for people with disabilities;

(ii) Rural development;

(iii) Appropriate technology;

(iv) Self-help initiatives of marginalized groups.

(e) NGO personnel and community members working on issues concerning:

(i) Disability and assistance to people with disabilities (from programme to individual levels);

(ii) Rural development;

(iii) Community action;

(iv) Technology;

(v) Empowerment of marginalized groups.

(f) People with disabilities involved in:

(i) Advocacy for protection of their rights or equalization of opportunity;

(ii) Empowerment of their peers;

(iii) Rehabilitation service delivery.

countries. Together with the Technical Workshop on the Indigenous Production and Distribution of Assistive Devices held in Madras,[1] India, in September 1995, the issuance of this publication is part of an ESCAP project to strengthen contact among personnel concerned with assistive devices and to raise the awareness of Governments in the region about the potential for meeting the demand for low-cost devices appropriate to users and their physical, cultural and social environments.

This publication focuses primarily on devices for people with lower-body locomotor disabilities (i.e., amputated or non-functional legs). Overall, this group currently has the most pressing unmet needs for appropriate devices. Devices for this group typically require the greatest amount of customization. Since the production of their devices is less easily standardized, it is often less profitable. The group's numbers are also large and increasing as a result of disabilities associated with land mines, armed conflict, as well as accidents related to sports, traffic and occupational hazards.

The publication does not deal at length with assistive devices for people with mental disorder or intellectual disabilities. Their needs, although important, are beyond the scope of this publication.

People who work with assistive devices in Asian and Pacific developing countries will find that this publication informs them about diverse approaches to production, and about producers and organizations they can contact. People whose work relates to other aspects of disability and rehabilitation issues should also find this publication useful, since assistive devices are a key aspect of all efforts to empower people with disabilities.

In addition, the publication should prove valuable for those who are involved with development or policy, in the Asia-Pacific region, in areas other than disability. It aims to demonstrate not only that the need for assistive devices in the region is urgent, but also that it can be met easily and at low cost through collaboration in a variety of fields.

Those researchers in applied science, mechanical and chemical engineers, and manufacturers who are not working directly with assistive devices may already be producing raw materials or parts that can be used in assistive devices. The examples contained in this publication demonstrate a potential and emerging market for these products.

Readers from or working in least-developed countries should not assume that their lack of resources is an impassable barrier in providing assistive devices for people with disabilities. Cambodia, classified as a least-developed country, has a highly developed system for producing and distributing assistive devices involving cooperation between NGOs and the Government.

---

[1] Officially renamed Chennai in 1996.

BOX 2: EXAMPLES OF ASSISTIVE DEVICES

(a) For people with locomotor disabilities:

   (i)   Orthoses;

   (ii)   Prosthetic limbs;

   (iii)   Wheelchairs of various types;

   (iv)   Tricycles, manual and motorized;

   (v)   Crutches;

   (vi)   Foot-drop spring shoes and other devices for people cured of leprosy.

(b) For people with hearing impairments:

   (i)   Hearing aids of different types (body-level, behind the ear, and in the ear canal);

   (ii)   Group hearing aids, such as loop-induction systems;

   (iii)   Communication boards;

   (iv)   Telephone amplifiers;

   (v)   Vibrating alarm clocks.

(c) For people with visual impairments:

   (i)   Braille slates;

   (ii)   Braille typewriters;

   (iii)   Computerized braille embossers;

   (iv)   Stylus;

   (v)   Braille paper;

   (vi)   White canes;

   (vii)   Braille geometry sets;

   (viii)   Pinhole masks;

   (ix)   Optical magnifiers for people with low vision.

(d) For people with multiple disabilities (e.g., cerebral palsy):

   (i)   Communication boards;

   (ii)   Rollators (walking devices with rollers);

   (iii)   Stimulation devices for toilet training;

   (iv)   Bolsters and balancing balls;

   (v)   Learning devices;

   (vi)   Adapted cutlery and crockery, such as spoons with special grips;

   (vii)   Positioning devices, such as special seating.

B. What are assistive devices?

Assistive devices (also known as technical aids, assistive equipment or assistive technology) are items that can directly enable people with disabilities to participate in the activities of daily life. People with disabilities may use assistive devices on their own or with the support of other people.

There are many types of assistive devices, all of which have a major role in improving people's lives. Communication boards help children with speech impairments to express themselves. Prosthetic feet allow amputees to walk. Braille writing slates enable people with visual disabilities to record information by themselves. Computers help people with visual impairments to communicate in text format. A loop-induction system makes it possible for someone with a hearing impairment to enjoy a musical performance.

Assistive devices reduce barriers between people with disabilities and their environments. In work, education or leisure, they bring about freedom of movement and greater ease of access. In some cases, assistive devices make it quicker and easier for people with disabilities to undertake activities that would otherwise be difficult; in others, they enable people to perform activities that would otherwise have been impossible.

Assistive devices have a central role in social policy. They empower people with disabilities to live with dignity as equal members of society and give them a new freedom and independence. That independence can reduce the cost of disabilities to individuals, to families and to society. Furthermore, the resulting enhancement in the quality of life of people with disabilities leads to the generation of new aspirations, new capacity to promote improvements in devices, and thus new innovations, in a continuous positive-feedback loop of innovation.

C. Evaluating assistive devices

The success of an assistive device is measured by whether its users actually use the device, do so in an effective and liberating way that gives them access to their environments, and are satisfied with the device in the long term. To achieve this goal, every assistive device in Asian and Pacific developing countries should have four primary qualities. Devices should be:

(a) Designed in consultation with users and their families in a way well suited to the users' diverse social and physical environments;

(b) Inexpensive to produce, purchase and maintain;

(c) Easy to use;

(d) Effective.

Devices originally designed for use in developed countries and imported directly from them are usually effective; i.e., they are capable of performing the functions for which they are intended.

However, they often lack the other three qualities. For example, a high-technology hearing aid may have the capability to provide beautifully clear sound to its user, but if its user must make a three-hour journey just to find new batteries, it will likely not be used once the batteries are dead. Under such circumstances, the capabilities of a device will be wasted. The best device that money can buy is not necessarily the best for users.

To ensure that a device has all four of these qualities requires a clear understanding of user needs. It also requires the direct involvement of potential users at each stage of design and development.

A list of features that give a device the four essential qualities (other than effectiveness) follows.

1. Devices designed to suit users and their environments

(a) Compatible with the users' aspirations, emotional needs, and ways of life;

(b) Compatible with the users' culture and local customs;

(c) Unobtrusive or attractive in appearance by local standards;

(d) Physically comfortable from users' perspectives;

(e) Sturdy enough that the users feel safe;

(f) Useful in a variety of situations;

(g) Durable, dependable and reliable, especially in rural areas, remote areas and rugged conditions;

(h) Compatible with the ground surface and other conditions of a user's physical environment.

2. Inexpensive devices

(a) Low in purchase price, so that a larger number of users than is presently the case can buy them, and Governments and/or NGOs can provide them free of charge or at subsidized rates;

(b) Easy (and affordable) to assemble or produce, for anyone with an interest in empowering people with disabilities, an aptitude for technical work, and appropriate short-term training;

(c) Easy and affordable to maintain, so that keeping the devices in working order requires minimal regular consumption of expensive or scarce resources;

(d) Amenable to repair with the use of locally available materials and technical skills, in or near the users' own communities.

3. Easy-to-use devices

(a) Easily understandable by users with limited exposure to technology;

(b) Easily moved from one place to another;

(c) Easy to operate without prolonged training or complex skills.

BOX 3: TWELVE PRINCIPLES OF ASSISTIVE-DEVICE PRODUCTION AND DISTRIBUTION

Participants in the Technical Workshop on the Indigenous Production and Distribution of Assistive Devices (held in Madras, India, 5-14 September 1995) agreed on 12 principles for the production and distribution of assistive devices. They are reproduced in their entirety in the Madras Workshop Proceedings, and are summarized here:

1. People with disabilities must define their own needs and be involved as equals in designing and testing assistive devices in a problem-solving approach to decision-making that empowers persons with disabilities.

2. The choice and design of assistive devices must suit the user's lifestyle, culture and environment.

3. People with disabilities should, when possible, be given priority for work and training related to assistive devices.

4. Devices must be made to fit users, not *vice versa*.

5. Support should be directed at strengthening small-scale community workshops that allow users' needs to be met by custom-made devices.

6. Local skills, materials and other resources should be used for production, repair and maintenance.

7. The design and production of assistive devices should be explained to local communities with limited exposure to sophisticated technology in such a way that they can make and adopt the devices.

8. Community-level innovation should be emphasized, and community collaboration with disabled persons and researchers encouraged.

9. Assistive devices should be seen as a part of the process of enabling people with disabilities to achieve their full potential;

10. Training and follow-up are essential for ensuring the continued appropriateness of assistive devices for users.

11. Decentralized production, achieved partly through widespread dissemination of knowledge and skills, is one way to meet user needs in remote areas;

12. Distribution of information on technologies and problem-solving skills supported by networking and exchange of products and training expertise, is as important as distribution of devices.

D. What is a disability?

The terms "disability", "handicap" and "impairment" are used in many different ways to cover a vast range of conditions. The most commonly cited definitions are those adopted by the World Health Organization (WHO) in 1980. In the context of health experience, WHO defined impairment, disability and handicap in the following ways:[2]

(a) An impairment is any loss or abnormality of psychological, physiological or anatomical structure or function;

(b) A disability is any restriction or lack (resulting from an impairment) of ability to perform an activity in the manner or within the range considered normal for a human being;

(c) A handicap is a disadvantage for a given individual, resulting from an impairment or a disability, that limits or prevents the fulfilment of a role that is normal (depending on age, sex, and social and cultural factors) for that individual.

People who wear glasses have a disability in that their sight is less than perfect. The availability of the glasses they need to see clearly, however, means that, for them, the disability of poor eyesight is not a handicap. It is the handicap, rather than the disability, which creates difficulty and must be dealt with. Assistive devices reduce, if not eliminate, the handicap.

---

2 United Nations, Department of International Economic and Social Affairs. *World Programme of Action concerning Disabled persons.* New York, 1983, p. 3.

When including marginalized people in the development process, it is essential to respond to their most urgent needs – as they see them.

BOX 4: CURRENT DEFINITIONS: IMPAIRMENT, DISABILITY AND HANDICAP*

Impairment: Any abnormality of psychological or physical *functions* or of *appearance*.

Disability: An interference with the *performance* of an activity by an individual in relation to the immediate environment.

Handicap: A societal disadvantage for a given individual that limits or prevents the performance of a *social role* or *participation*.

In general, impairments result in disabilities, which result in handicaps of social integration. However, the relationship is not necessarily causal or unidirectional.

Terms:	Impairment	Disability	Handicap
Levels:	Organ	Person	Society
Disablement:	Body structure/ function	Activities	Roles
Traumatic Injury:	Loss of an eye	Limited depth perception	Unable to obtain a driving licence

Example	Impairment	Disability	Handicap
Attention Deficit/ Hyperactivity Disorder	*Minimal brain damage, distracti- bility, problems in concentration, high activity level, writing difficulty*	*Attention deficit (learning disabi- lity), difficulties completing tasks and waiting for turn in group activities*	*Viewed/labelled by others as "a problem" and excluded from activities considered normal for peers of the same age and family background, living in the same community*

* **Source:** Excerpted from information provided by Dr. T. Bedirhan Ustun, Senior Scientist, World Health Organization Division of Mental Health and Prevention of Substance Abuse, and Coordinator of the second revision of the International Classification of Impairments, Disabilities and Handicap (ICIDH), WHO, 1980. The ICIDH is being updated and the second revision is scheduled for 1999. For further information, contact Dr. Ustun: 20 Avenue Appia, CH-1211, Geneva 27, Switzerland; Fax: +41 22 791 4885; Tel: +41 22 791 3609; Email: Ustun@who.ch

E. People with disabilities in Asian and Pacific developing countries

1. Poverty and other causes of disabilities

The majority of people with disabilities are likely to be poor. The following are among common poverty-related causes of disability (subdivided by type of disability):

(a) For locomotor disabilities: Leprosy; poliomyelitis (polio). In India, polio is the single largest contributor to the prevalence of locomotor disability; in heavily mined Afghanistan, a Handicap International survey found that polio caused more disabilities than land mines. Furthermore, poverty reduces options and compels many to risk disability resulting from the need to work in mined areas.

The poor are especially vulnerable.

(b) For hearing disabilities: Rubella during pregnancy; iodine deficiency and diseases such as meningitis, hepatitis, typhoid or measles in early childhood; ear infections at any time in life.

(c) For visual disabilities: Vitamin A deficiency (in children); leprosy; and cataract (without access to surgery and rehabilitation).

(d) For multiple disabilities (e.g., cerebral palsy): Maternal stress, unsafe birth practices and perinatal trauma associated with conditions of poverty.

Furthermore, the ensuing disabilities have more serious consequences for the poor, who have limited access to rehabilitation services and assistive devices. Even when poor families can theoretically afford assistive devices, they may still assign a lower priority to using their scarce resources on the purchase of devices than to food and shelter. The poor are also more likely to live in an environment whose handicapping features are overwhelming.

The aforementioned causes are all preventable with proper use of resources. Developed countries have all but eliminated them, and many developing countries of the ESCAP region are making progress toward their elimination. In Pakistan, for example, there is a campaign to immunize all Pakistani children against polio within the next five years.

Furthermore, absolute poverty can be a more severe limitation on life activities than disability *per se*. Obtaining a brailler will be of low priority for a blind person who faces death from starvation. All who are concerned with disability issues must bear in mind that assistive devices are only one element of a national disability strategy. Poverty alleviation and provision of adequate health services are central.

Nevertheless, poverty alleviation itself requires the availability of appropriate assistive devices. To fight poverty, all the members of a family, including those with disabilities, must contribute to the family economy. Without the appropriate devices, family members with disabilities may be a burden. With appropriate devices, along with changes in access and social attitudes, they can contribute productively. For this reason, in the rehabilitation of poor people with disabilities, it is especially critical that the devices provided facilitate their participation in activities of economic value to their families.

Although poverty is a major cause of disability, many other causes exist, and anyone can acquire a disability at any point in life. People in the middle and upper classes of the Asia-Pacific region are not immune.

Among older people, hearing and vision can deteriorate to the point where they become impossible without assistive devices. A stroke can cause paraplegia. A fall can cause limb damage that does not heal.

Among young people, accidents involving motorized vehicles or outdoor activities can cause spinal cord injury leading to paralysis. Regular and prolonged exposure to noise in mass entertainment venues may lead to hearing impairment.

Newborn babies can have genetic disabilities, even if their parents do not. In addition, although perinatal birth trauma is most common among the poor, it can lead to disabilities even in babies born to wealthy families.

Two other causes of disabilities that are uncommon in developed countries exist in developing countries of the ESCAP region. One is the existence of uncleared anti-personnel landmines in Afghanistan, Cambodia, Islamic Republic of Iran, Myanmar and Viet Nam, and unexploded ordnance (UXO) in the Lao People's Democratic Republic, which regularly destroys life and limb. Over 10 million mines remain uncleared in Afghanistan. In Cambodia, one in every 236 people is an amputee because of mines. In Myanmar, over 1500 people every year are fitted with artificial limbs as a result of landmine explosions. Many mine victims never receive medical attention at all.[3]

The second cause is poor adherence to safety measures in mechanized farming. In manual farming, operators can stop machines quickly and easily when a problem arises. In mechanized farming, however, control switches may not be within easy reach of the operator or safety guards may not be in position, leading to serious injuries which result in disabilities.

---

[3] "Uncleared Land Mines: the Scope of the Problem in Africa, Asia, the Middle East, the Americas, and Europe", *UNIDIR Newsletter*, No. 28/29, Dec. 1994/May 1995, p. 47.

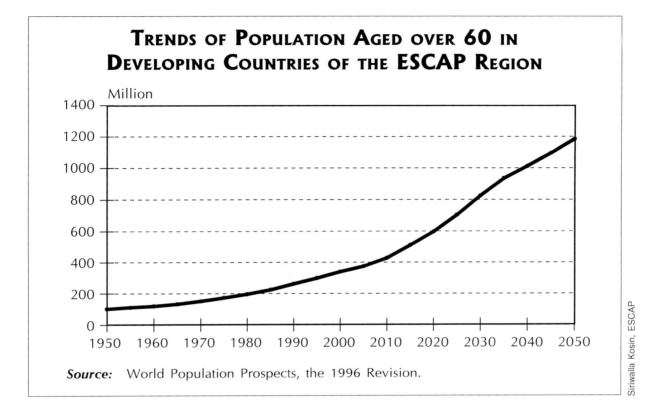

TRENDS OF POPULATION AGED OVER 60 IN DEVELOPING COUNTRIES OF THE ESCAP REGION

Million

Source: World Population Prospects, the 1996 Revision.

Siriwalla Kosin, ESCAP

The need for assistive devices in the ESCAP region will increase with the rapid ageing of societies.

13

Anyone can acquire a disability at any point in life.

In both these cases, victims will clearly need assistive devices. Demining programmes, support for campaigns to ban landmines, and better safety standards for farm equipment and training can, however, reduce this need in the future.

Violence at home and in public places may also result in disability. When violence involves the use of guns and other lethal weapons, survivors are often permanently disabled by spinal cord injuries.

2. Levels of need for assistive devices

There are no firm data on the number of people with disabilities in developing countries of the ESCAP region. Most developing countries have not conducted any comprehensive surveys on the subject. This poses problems for both planning and evaluating programmes to provide assistive devices. Without such surveys, people will neither know what assistive devices are needed nor know how much of that need is being met.

In countries that have disability statistics, the number of people with disabilities, expressed as a percentage of the country's total population, varies from 1.85 per cent in Thailand to 10 per cent in Pakistan.[4] It must, however, be stressed that such figures represent differences in methodology or definitions of "disability" as much as differences in the population itself. The figure of 1.85 per cent for Thailand, for example, comes

---

[4] Pakistan and Thailand country papers, in Part II: Madras Workshop Proceedings.

14

from interview and questionnaire surveys conducted in 1991. A 1991-1992 Thai study, however, used physical examination of the population as its method and concluded instead that 6.3 per cent of the population – more than three times as many – had disabilities. Furthermore, unlike the survey study, the physical-examination study did not examine people for the presence of intellectual disabilities. It is estimated that, if the survey had included them, the figure found would likely have been around 8.1 per cent instead.[5] It is likely that the latter method is more accurate, but it requires a more comprehensive definition of disability and concomitant allocation of resources.

These figures demonstrate the difficulty of obtaining a realistic estimate of the number of people with disabilities, especially in rural areas. At the macro level, numbers are important for planning a coordinated system to supply assistive devices. An effective assistive-device service, however, can only be provided through a network with delivery channels at the micro level, channels which can capture an understanding of the needs of every disabled person. This is more easily achieved by local authorities and NGOs than national, provincial or state Governments.

About 90 per cent of China's people with disabilities need at least one assistive device.[6] A survey in Viet Nam

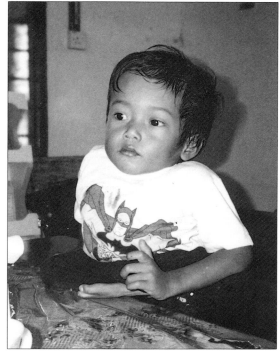

Even without firm disability data, efforts must continue to improve services.

asking people with locomotor disabilities about their needs found that 67 per cent required an assistive device.[7] In Thailand, 66,712 people needed at least one device in 1995: about 83 per cent of the total registered population of people with disabilities, numbering around 80,000. The government registration roster does not, however, include all Thai people with disabilities. Thailand's experience further demonstrates that much of the demand for assistive devices is not currently being met. The Thai Central

---

[5] Information provided in July 1997 by the Department of Public Welfare, Ministry of Labour and Social Welfare, Royal Thai Government.

[6] China country paper, in Part II: Madras Workshop Proceedings.

[7] Ho Nhu Hai, "Motor Disabled People in Rural Areas of Vietnam", paper presented to the Round Table Meeting on the Integration of Disabled People in Agricultural and Agro-Industry Systems, held by the Food and Agriculture Organization of the United Nations, 13-15 May 1997, Bangkok.

Government Budget for 1995 provided funds for only about 20,000 people with disabilities.[8]

As a country undergoes rapid economic and social change, the patterns of disabilities in that country will also change rapidly. In Thailand, for example, the number of people with disabilities resulting from polio has decreased in recent years, but the number with disabilities resulting from traffic accidents has increased.[9]

The unmet need for assistive devices is usually greatest in rural and remote areas. Sometimes, this is a result of a greater overall need; more often, it is because production and distribution are concentrated in capitals and other major urban centres. In Indonesia, for example, the vast majority of device producers are on Java island and few high-quality devices are available elsewhere. In Fiji, the only sources of devices are in Suva.

It is wrong to assume that the need for specific devices is distributed evenly among or within geographical regions. Needs differ in relation to variations in the incidence of disabilities, local conditions and individual differences. The need for orthoses, for example, is greatest in places where poliomyelitis and cerebral palsy are major causes of locomotor disabilities. Furthermore, even small geographical areas may differ greatly within themselves in the needs they face. Workers for Handicap International observed a case in southern Thailand where ten blind people lived in one village while a neighbouring village had no blind inhabitants at all.

3. Women and girls with disabilities

Most women and girls with disabilities in every community, whether urban or rural, experience triple discrimination from being female, disabled

Local improvisation until an artificial limb is obtained.

---

8   Thailand country paper, in Part II: Madras Workshop Proceedings.

9   Health Research Institute/National Health Foundation, Ministry of Public Health, Royal Thai Government, 1992.

and poor. As women's needs generally receive lower priority than men's, so women with disabilities receive a lower priority for obtaining assistive devices. According to the United Nations Children's Fund (UNICEF), women and children together receive less than 20 per cent of rehabilitation services, including the provision of prostheses and orthoses.[10]

Furthermore, with few exceptions, little effort has been made to obtain the views of women and girls with disabilities concerning assistive devices or to incorporate their views in the design and production of the devices; as a result, the devices often do not suit them. For example, in many parts of the region, food is prepared at ground level. In order to cook, many women with post-polio paralysis drag themselves on the ground or use a simple wooden support block, rather than use a wheelchair. Ground mobility devices (see the Technical Specifications Supplement) are a useful way to deal with this problem. For another example, above-knee prostheses are difficult to adjust for pregnant women, and little research has been done into designs that are more suitable for pregnant women.

Little effort has been made to incorporate the views of women and girls with disabilities in the development of assistive devices.

4. Older people and children with disabilities

Older people and children with disabilities require special attention. Older people are likely to acquire disabilities as a result of old age. Many resist being labelled as "disabled", and are therefore reluctant to use assistive devices, even though the devices could significantly improve their lives. They are also more susceptible than others to multiple disabilities. The need for different types of assistive devices, or for devices specially

---

10   UNICEF, *Relief and Rehabilitation of Traumatized Children in War Situations.* Paper submitted for the World Summit on Children, 1990.

A child should not be made to use a wheelchair designed for an adult.

R. Saha

designed for people with multiple disabilities, will therefore be higher among them.

Children require devices whose size and ease of manipulation suit them. A child should not be made to use a wheelchair designed for an adult, but this remains a common occurrence. Furthermore, growing children require regular attention to ensure that they are not constrained by devices that they have outgrown. For example, a three-year-old child will outgrow an orthosis in a few months' time. Unless the old orthosis is updated or replaced, the child's development will be hampered.

Devices that do not fit a child's needs can do more harm than good. For example, a child who tends to walk with bent knees may topple over backwards when wearing an orthosis whose ankles are fixed at 90 degrees. Bracing designed to correct the effects of spasticity in children with cerebral palsy may occasionally trigger even more spasticity.

Well-designed orthoses can be of great benefit to children with cerebral palsy and other disabilities, but it is crucial that the devices be approached in an experimental, open-ended, trial-and-error way where each child's feelings, responses and concerns are made central to the problem-solving process.

Although there are exceptions, children below the age of three years are generally the group most vulnerable to polio. Paralysis caused by polio at this early age often hinders children from walking properly. For the development of their full potential (physical, mental and social), rehabilitation must begin as early as possible. This is even more so in the case of children with disabilities resulting from birth trauma, as they may have multiple disabilities.

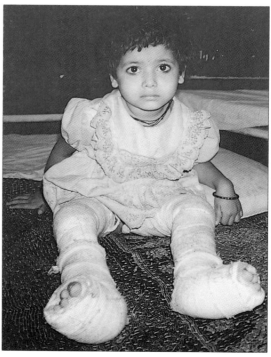

Rehabilitation must begin as early as possible.

18

CHAPTER II

ASSISTIVE DEVICES AND INCLUSION IN SOCIETY

The initiatives of the Asian and Pacific Decade of Disabled Persons aim to foster an environment which will provide equal opportunities for people with disabilities and enhance their options for full participation in society. Assistive devices built into the environments of people with disabilities help achieve this objective by enabling disabled people to participate in mainstream community life, including employment, education, family activities and recreation.

For example, a proper lighting system and strong colour contrast in the built environment will help people with low vision to perform tasks better. Such a lighting system would be additional to their use of magnifying devices. People in wheelchairs who have reachers (see Technical Specifications Supplement) or extended hooks will find it easier to take things from shelves at a height. Blind people must currently rely on sighted people to read their own bank statements. With the advent of small computerized braille embossers, it should be possible to issue braille bank statements to blind customers. However, for this to occur, banks must adopt a policy to this effect and bank employees must be persuaded to implement the policy as a matter of course.

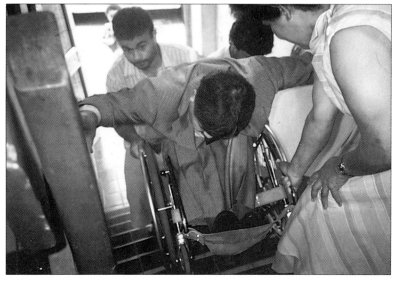

Assistive devices, an accessible environment and positive attitudes – one without the others does not suffice.

A. Access

Having appropriate assistive devices *per se* is not enough to enable people with disabilities to participate in mainstream development programmes and community life. Assistive devices must be considered together with access to the built environment and a social milieu that welcomes the participation of persons with disabilities. An integrated solution is required to produce a significant enhancement in the participation of people with disabilities in society. Without accessible environments and positive attitudes, users of assistive devices continue to face similar difficulties to those they would face without assistive devices.

On the other hand, making environments both physically and socially accessible can be a futile effort if assistive devices are not available. Installing ramps to make a school accessible for wheelchair users will help little if students who require wheelchairs do not have them. Furthermore, no matter how accessible the environment and how useful their devices, people with disabilities will still be excluded from society without progress in the elimination of discriminatory practices.

The built environment is composed of buildings and other physical structures, the spaces around and between those structures (however far the distance between them may be), and the infrastructure which makes it possible for people to move to, from and within built areas.

A non-handicapping, or barrier-free, environment is one to which people with disabilities have access. Access to a space in the built environment means that people can get to, from and around the space and use it in a safe and convenient way. Conversely, a handicapping environment is one which is unsafe, inconvenient or impossible for people with disabilities to move around in. Handicapping environments are the prevailing situation in many Asian and Pacific developing countries.

Features which should be accessible to people with disabilities include entrances, exits, door handles, corridors, toilets, escape routes, refreshment facilities, elevators, staircases and parking. Ways to improve access include installing water coolers, telephones and counters at wheelchair height, to enable wheelchair users to use them without assistance. Braille markings in elevators enable blind people to operate them independently. Similarly, a change in the texture of the ground near an elevator enables blind people to clearly identify the elevator doorway.[11]

Different buildings and spaces in Asian and Pacific developing countries must be made accessible in different ways. In South-East Asia and in the Pacific, for example, houses are often built on stilts. The height of these houses varies from three to five metres. Stairs or ladders are used for entry and exit. If stairs are the only entrance and exit, a person in a wheelchair cannot go in or out. A hoisting system using pulleys and cables is useful to transport people with lower-limb disabilities or cerebral palsy.

---

[11]   See United Nations, ESCAP. *Promotion of Non-Handicapping Physical Environments for Disabled Persons: Guidelines* (ST/ESCAP/ 1492), New York, 1995, for further discussion of access issues.

Thus appropriate assistive devices, together with an accessible built environment and positive attitudes, significantly enhance the inclusion of people with disabilities in society.

B. Education

Children with disabilities often require assistive devices to participate in education. Sometimes, lack of one assistive device is all that separates a child from participation and inclusion in a regular school. With the right device, a child may not have to attend a special school, segregated from peers without disabilities.

People with disabilities may not be able to realize their right to an education without assistive devices. People with upper-body locomotor disabilities require assistive devices to write, and children with lower-body locomotor disabilities require them in order to attend classes.

People with hearing disabilities require assistive devices to hear their teachers and participate in class. However, services for assessing hearing impairments, prescribing hearing aids and producing them for distribution to people with hearing impairments are limited.

People with low vision require assistive devices to read notes, books and blackboards, and very few have them. The International Council for Education of People with Visual Impairment (ICEVI) estimates that 90 per cent of the world's people with visual disabilities do not have access to an

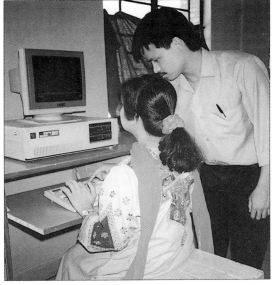

Computer technology helps break communication barriers between hearing and deaf persons.

education.[12] Blind people can receive the great benefits of braille-related assistive devices such as embossers and slates only if they have learned how to read braille. Currently, the majority of blind people in Asian and Pacific developing countries have not been enabled to do so.

An inexpensive way to distribute assistive devices in education is for a government ministry or department to maintain a stock of assistive devices to lend to students. When the students complete their studies or outgrow their devices, they may return these devices to the ministry or department. This approach is not suitable for the most user-specific devices, such as prosthetic limbs.

---

12 William G. Brohier, "President's Message", *The Educator*, Vol. X, No. 1 (Winter 1997), p. 4.

Teachers should have a basic working knowledge of different types of childhood disabilities and the corresponding types of assistive devices, in order to address the needs of children with disabilities in their classrooms. This would put teachers in a better position to discuss children's needs for devices, in school and home-based activities, with parents and health workers.

C. Employment

1. Agriculture and other rural employment

People with disabilities in rural areas should be employed in their own surroundings unless the reasons for doing otherwise are compelling. For example, a person who has been trained in technical skills may prefer to work in an industry rather than getting into traditional trades. Others may choose to migrate to urban centres to find more remunerative employment. If people themselves do not choose to leave their rural communities, however, they should not be forced to do so because of lack of options associated with their disabilities.

It is therefore crucial that rural environments be made accessible. Many employment options in rural areas are open to everyone, including people with disabilities. Such options are found, for example, in agriculture, horticulture, animal husbandry, handicrafts, carpentry, tailoring, blacksmithy and mechanical or electrical repair work.

On-site modifications to workplaces are often, but not always, essential. This depends on the type of disability and type of work. The modifications may be as simple as lowering the height of a work surface or lengthening everyday gardening tools so that wheelchair users can use them. Whether or not modifications are essential, assistive devices must be suitability designed, modified and produced for the tasks involved. Lower-limb amputees working in rice fields, for example, must have prostheses designed in such a way that they can wear it to work in the fields.

Tractors and harvesters can be adapted for use by people with disabilities. This may require small modifications in the machines, such as adding one or more steps to the driver's seat for people wearing orthoses or prostheses. Modification of the height and position of the seat, or the replacement of foot controls with hand controls, may also be required.

Association of People with Disability, Bangalore, India

A blind and mobility-impaired person who has developed his gift for gardening.

22

2. Employment in the manufacturing and service sectors

Many service jobs available in Asian and Pacific developing countries, such as those of bookkeepers and clerks, do not necessarily call for special devices. Technical jobs may sometimes require on-site modifications to enable disabled people to work on machines or to improve their efficiency. Generally, the layout of assembly lines and machines does not take the needs of people with disabilities into consideration.

Many work tools for use in the household and in industry are unsuitable for people with certain disabilities but can be made suitable through simple "universal" designs; i.e., small modifications that make the tools safer and more user-friendly for everyone, and especially people with disabilities. These include nail and screw holders for people with visual disabilities, vise grip attachments for prostheses, and braille rulers.[13]

With a prosthesis, farming continues after a below-knee amputation.

Cyril Siriwardene

The built-in safety of many high-technology machines is an asset for disabled people, as they can safely and easily operate these machines. When replacing existing machines, industries and workshops in the region, especially public-sector ones, should install machines based on principles of universal design. They may highlight this aspect in tender notices and purchase queries for new machines.

In the Veterans International production workshop in Phnom Penh, wheelchair users are able to operate an injection moulding machine because the bed of the machine has been lowered to match the height of their wheelchairs. The Sheltered Workshop, a vocational training centre in Klang, Malaysia, has sewing machines whose height can be adjusted to suit the height of individual wheelchair users.

Adaptations to machines are extremely important for people with visual impairments. Some examples follow.

To enable blind people to perform precision measurement tasks, micrometers with braille attachments are available. At Bharat Earth Movers Ltd. in Bangalore, India, a blind person is engaged in a

---

13   For further details and examples, see Human Resources Development Canada. *Tips, Tools and Techniques: Home Maintenance and Hobbycraft, People with Disabilities and Seniors* Ottawa, 1995.

BOX 5: ABDUL MATIN MAHABUB'S STORY*

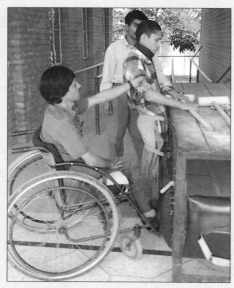

Abdul Matin Mahabub in wheel-chair at work.

Name:	Abdul Matin Mahabub
Religion:	Islam
Age:	38 years
Home:	Chapain, Savar, Dhaka
Education:	S.S.C. from Muslimabad High School, Comilla, Bangladesh
Career:	13 years at the Centre for the Rehabilitation of the Paralysed (CRP), Savar, Dhaka
Current Post:	Head of the CRP Occupational Therapy Department

In 1980, while working as an electrician in the Power Development Board (PDB), I fell from an electricity pole and broke my back. I came to CRP for treatment and spent three months in the Centre. After treatment I returned to my village. Two years later, the CRP social worker brought me back to the Centre and arranged training in weaving, radio and T.V. repair and poultry rearing. This training lasted one year. Then the CRP appointed me as a Junior Occupational Therapy Assistant. Six years later I was promoted. I worked as a Senior Occupational Therapy Assistant for three years. Now I am working at CRP as the Head of its Occupational Therapy Department.

I, along with other staff of the Department, provide services without which certain essential needs of the patients would be neglected. Our Department is involved in the provision of mobility aids to the patients. The aids are made of locally available materials which are designed to be adaptable to both rural and urban terrains. I assess for needs regarding wheelchair equipment and special splints and give treatment and training for functional independence.

Now I am interested in taking part in workshops and training which will help my Department to further develop. I feel that exposure to others working in similar areas as myself and to new ideas on mobility aids and equipment for disabled people would allow my Department to improve the service we are offering to our patients and disabled people in Bangladesh.

I feel that my own experience and background in working in the field of occupational therapy in Bangladesh would also be helpful to others taking part in similar training.

* **Source:** Abdul Matin Mahabub, CRP, Savar, Bangladesh.

drilling job. He uses a jig to fix the job and then drills a hole at the right place. In another factory in India, a blind person operates a small machine with a checking mechanism. He can close and open the chuck for polishing watch dials. The machine is preset for the depth of finish and the blind person has to ensure proper fixing of the job in the chuck before performing the actual operation.[14]

Assistive devices such as closed-circuit television with magnification facilities, reading machines, computers with large-print displays, speech synthesizers and braille embossers can enable blind people and people with low vision to manage offices.

To encourage open employment, Governments could provide such devices to any industry recruiting blind people. Several developed countries have this policy. Under such a policy, the Government concerned normally requires the return of such devices if the blind person in question leaves the position and his or her replacement is not blind.

In inspection and quality-control workshops in industry, blind people can be very effective when a "go" / "no go" decision is involved. In such cases, the analog output of a measurement gauge can be converted into an audio output to indicate whether a part has passed the quality requirement. Many such jobs are

---

[14] R. Saha and others, "Technology and Employment Opportunities for Disabled in Industry", *Indian Journal of Disability and Rehabilitation*, January-June 1992.

available in large industries. Work sites need to be studied carefully on a continuous basis in order to support more such adaptations.

People with hearing impairments can use telephones which incorporate flashing lights to draw their attention to incoming calls. Similarly, all emergency signs may be coupled with flashing lights.

R. Saha

Appropriate devices, training and work site adaptations would expand employment options.

For various reasons, many people with disabilities who are employed do not use the applicable assistive devices. This makes their jobs tiring and reduces their efficiency. At the time of recruitment, the need of people with disabilities for assistive devices must be properly assessed. Subsequently, arrangements must be made to provide the devices that will enable them to perform their tasks to the best of their ability.

There are many examples of on-site modifications in industries, adaptations to existing devices and design and development of new devices. However, these experiences have not been properly documented for others to use in their own situations. A document highlighting such experiences would be helpful.

D. Recreation

People with hearing impairments find it difficult to enjoy mass audio entertainment. In an enclosed entertainment venue, it is possible to enclose a small area with a loop-induction system so that people with hearing impairments within it can hear voices and sounds without ambient noise. A loop-induction system comprises of a microphone, an amplifier and a loop (a conducting wire encircling the enclosure). The sound of music or the voices of actors are converted into electromagnetic signals. The signals are carried to the loop. A pickup coil fitted in a hearing aid picks up the electromagnetic signals and the receiver in the ear converts this into comprehensible speech or music. Since the hearing aid does not pick up actual sound signals,

BOX 6: SPORTS WHEELCHAIRS

Topong Kulkhanchit

To participate fully in community life, different types of wheelchairs are required.

The Wheelchair Maintenance Clinic in Nonthaburi, Thailand (see Box 8) has modified the design of sports wheelchairs used in developed countries. Sports wheelchairs use high-technology materials, including aluminium alloy and titanium, to make them light and easy to manoeuvre.

The Clinic is currently concentrating on increasing the production of sports wheelchairs for the Seventh Far East and South Pacific Games for Disabled Persons (FESPIC Games), scheduled to be held in Bangkok in January 1999. The Clinic imports main and castor wheels from Taiwan Province of China. The other parts are all produced in Thailand.

it receives no ambient noise, ensuring good quality of sound. Other devices include TV listening devices, which allow television sound to be heard at a comfortable level by people with hearing impairments, while not disturbing others in the room.

Recreational items for people with visual impairments include braille playing cards and an audible ball ("beeperball") for ball games. Many of these devices, especially electronic ones, are not available in most developing countries of the ESCAP region. In places where they are produced, they have limited distribution.

Light wheelchairs with a wide base (sports wheelchairs) are important to enable their users to play ball games, such as basketball or tennis, and to dance. This design of wheelchair is, however, more expensive.

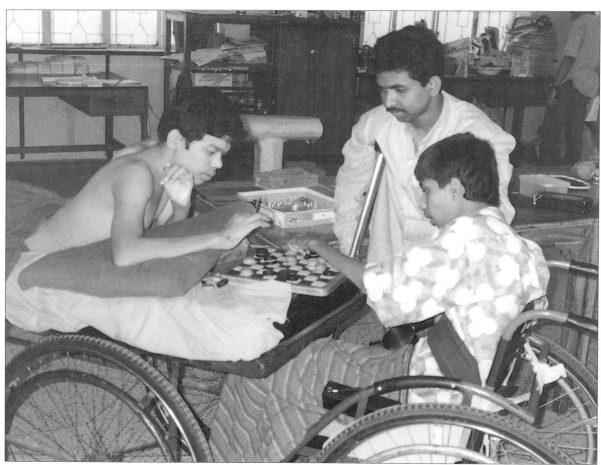

Recreation too is an integral part of living.

CHAPTER III

DESIGN AND PRODUCTION OF SPECIFIC DEVICES

A. Lower-limb prostheses

Below-knee amputations are the most common type of amputation; above-knee amputations are the next most common. To produce below-knee (BK) prostheses, a production unit must have the necessary parts, such as pylons and prosthetic feet, and the facilities and expertise to make sockets and shanks. The basic components of a BK prosthesis are the socket, the shank and the foot-ankle system. A shank is a structural component of a prosthesis which connects the socket to the foot-ankle system and transfers the load of body weight to the foot and the floor.

There are two types of prostheses: exoskeletal (or crustacean) and endoskeletal. Exoskeletal prostheses are the most commonly used in the region. Their shanks are on the outside, typically made of wood, thermoplastic or polyester resin. The inside is usually filled with wood. Endoskeletal prostheses have the most lifelike appearance, but require careful maintenance. Their shank is on the inside. It is a central tube, called the pylon, which is usually made of aluminum. It is covered in foam or polypropylene and encased in a latex or fabric stocking for cosmetic purposes. These prostheses are available in many developing countries of the ESCAP region, although they are all imported.

Three different materials are most commonly used in the making of BK prostheses: aluminium alloys, polypropylene and titanium. Polypropylene has three advantages over aluminium: it is much lighter; it is cheaper; and setting up production facilities may be easier for it than for aluminium.

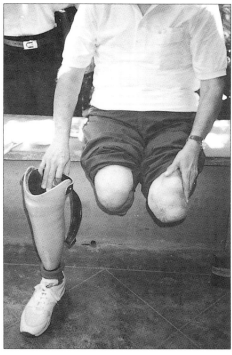

Bilateral below-knee amputation and exoskeletal below-knee resin prosthesis.

Titanium is extensively used in China for making expensive high-quality pylons, which are attached to the prosthetic foot and socket through an attachment plate. This considerably increases the strength and reduces the weight of a prosthesis. Fabrication of titanium parts is difficult, however, as special equipment is required to process the metal in an oxygen-free atmosphere.

Some countries, including Thailand and Viet Nam, have attempted to use computer-aided socket design and manufacture. The main difference is that the computer-aided technique does not require that a plaster-of-Paris (POP) cast of the stump be taken and a negative mould be produced in order to make the positive mould. Instead, a positive POP cast is directly made by digitizing the shape and the size of the stump through computerized scanning. Unfortunately, the expertise needed to use the method is not yet widely available in developing countries of the ESCAP

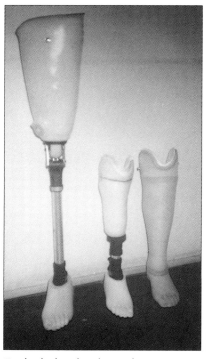

Endoskeletal above-knee prosthesis (left), polypropylene (PP) below-knee prosthesis (centre) and modular system endoskeletal below-knee resin prosthesis (right).

region, and so the application of the technique has thus far had limited success.

The alignment of prostheses and orthoses should ideally be established by well-trained professionals. However, most Asian and Pacific developing countries do not have sufficient numbers of trained prosthetists to establish alignment in this way.

The most common BK prosthesis now in use is the patellar-tendon-bearing (PTB) prosthesis. The shank of a PTB prosthesis is usually made of wood, but its socket is made of polyester resin or (increasingly) polypropylene. The socket

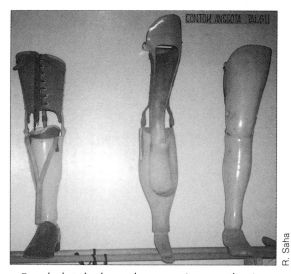

Exoskeletal above-knee resin prosthesis.

is made using a mould based on a plaster cast of the stump. (See the Technical Specifications Supplement for further details.)

The Jaipur prosthesis, a type of exoskeletal prosthesis which was originally made of aluminium, has a socket that is open on both ends. This makes it easier for the prosthesis to fit stumps of non-optimal size, common in Asian and Pacific developing countries. Its open socket is also more suitable for hot climates than a total-contact socket. It is, however, less suitable for wet climates

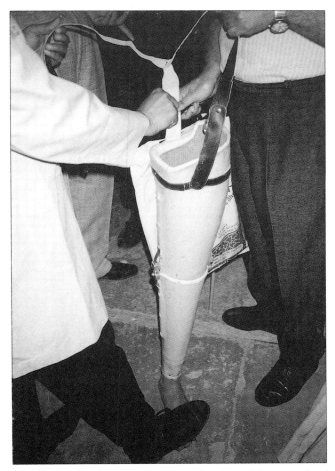

Exoskeletal above-knee prosthesis with attached leather suspension belt.

where water and moisture can enter. Jaipur prostheses generally include a Jaipur Foot as their foot component, although some Jaipur prostheses use different kinds of feet.

People cured of leprosy should not receive a prosthesis with this type of open-ended socket. As peripheral anaesthesia often extends up to the knee, they need a perfect fit that does not require sensory feedback. (See Box 7 for further detail.)

The initial work on providing prostheses in Cambodia started with an aluminium Jaipur prosthesis. An NGO in Thailand provides these aluminium prostheses through a mobile workshop in rural and remote areas.

The aluminium Jaipur prosthesis remains the least expensive and the easiest to produce. It does, however, have some major drawbacks. First, it is less physically attractive than most other prostheses. Second, as aluminium absorbs heat, many users in a hot climate find it too hot to be comfortable. Third, the fact that it is produced manually makes alignment difficult. It is far easier to adjust the alignment of modular, endoskeletal prostheses. Poor alignment can, in turn, make it awkward to walk with this prosthesis. As a result of these difficulties, few agencies in Cambodia and Thailand still make it.

The design of the Jaipur prosthesis has been considerably changed by using high-density

BOX 7: DEVICES FOR PEOPLE AFFECTED BY LEPROSY

Leprosy has two aspects: loss of motor function and loss of peripheral (protective) sensation. Loss of sensation means that people with leprosy cannot sense heat or pain from mild injuries, and sometimes even severe ones. As a result, they must exercise special care and use protective coverings, handles and clothing. The injuries that go unnoticed can easily become infected. If these injuries are not attended to in time, they may lead to the loss of fingers and toes. The loss of these motor functions makes it difficult for people affected by leprosy to engage in many productive activities.

Oven gloves, conventional gloves and mittens can protect hands from injury. Therapeutic splints are made to correct contractures of the interphalangeal joints as an aid to mobilizing exercises, massage and other physiotherapy procedures. These splints are made with polyvinyl chloride (PVC) sheets and velcro straps. Some rehabilitation programmes also use soft PVC hose pipes, which are cut lengthwise into two slightly curved gutters. These gutters are attached using velcro straps, sticking plaster or bandages.

People cured of leprosy who have "foot drop" require functional devices to achieve a normal gait. Foot-drop spring shoes are helpful until a surgical correction is carried out. Protective devices are critical for feet without sensation because the foot is the body part most vulnerable to injury.

Footwear should fit closely without being tight. Socks are necessary to reduce the frictional trauma from the upper portion of shoes. Leather is a good material to use in shoes for people with leprosy or cured of it, because it absorbs sweat and moulds itself to make a better fit over time. Since many people affected by leprosy are poor, however, they cannot afford leather shoes.

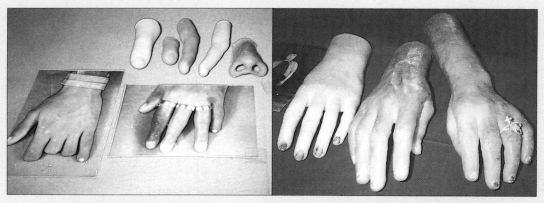

Some assistive devices (artificial hands, fingers, nose) for people affected by leprosy.

Source: Schieffelin Leprosy Research and Training Centre and Hospital, Karigiri, Tamil Nadu, India.

polyethylene (HDPE) to make both the socket and the shank. The HDPE is available in the form of pipes designed for irrigating rice fields. It is thus easily available in many developing countries in the region. The Technical Specifications Supplement provides detailed instructions on how to make the HDPE Jaipur prosthesis. Although the HDPE prosthesis is generally an improvement over the aluminium design, it requires an oven and a facility for taking a plaster cast, which the aluminium prosthesis does not.

The conventional above-knee (AK) prosthesis is made of willow wood, with a socket carved in a wooden shank. This type of prosthesis is still in use, but the number of users is quickly decreasing. Its heavy weight is a disadvantage. The newer thermoplastic or resin prostheses are lighter and easier to make.

The shape of the socket is crucial for comfort and functionality. The socket should allow blood circulation without being loose. Quadrilateral sockets are nearly rectangular in shape when viewed from the top. They are among the most commonly used sockets in the region, as they provide almost total contact with the limb.

For active amputees with good blood circulation, a close fit between the stump and the socket can create a suction that holds the prosthesis in place. In this kind of socket, called a suction socket, nothing is worn on the stump. When blood circulation is poor, a sock is worn over the stump and the socket is held in place by a belt around the pelvic area. This latter type is the most common type of socket in the region.

B. Upper-limb prostheses

In most Asian and Pacific developing countries, only a few rehabilitation centres produce prostheses for upper limbs (arms and hands). In Afghanistan, for example, upper-limb prostheses are not provided except when a user requests one for cosmetic reasons or for young bilateral upper limb amputees to enhance functional independence.[15]

The basic components of an upper-limb prosthesis are:

(a) Socket;

(b) Wrist unit;

(c) Terminal device or hand;

(d) Power transmission system;

(e) Forearm;

(f) Arm section;

(g) Elbow mechanism (for above-elbow amputees);

(h) Suspension system.

Leather or nylon cords transmit tension force, generated by movement of the shoulder, to operate the terminal device or the hand. The elbow is not always needed, as prostheses are most

---

[15] Thomas Berhane, "Sandy Gall's Afghanistan Appeal: Orthopaedic Workshop and Physiotherapy Programmes for Afghans", in Report of ISPO Consensus Conference on Appropriate Prosthetic Technology for Developing Countries, Phnom Penh, June 5-10, 1995.

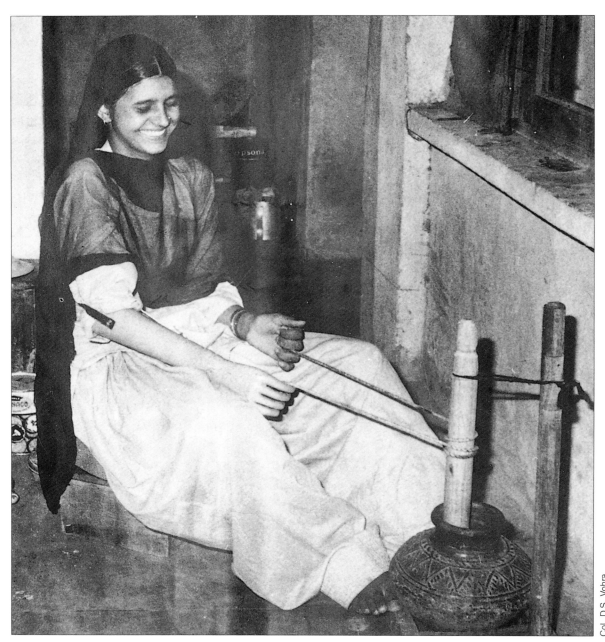

Col. D.S. Vohra

Churning milk with a below-elbow prosthesis.

commonly prescribed for people with below-elbow amputations, whose elbow function is retained. The function of the suspension system is to hold the prosthesis in position during all of its possible movements.

The terminal device is a centrally important part of the prosthesis, since it provides replacement of the limb's most important function, prehension or ability to grasp an object. The hand is one of the most intricate organs of

34

the human body. As such, it poses a serious challenge to the designing of prostheses meant to replace the function of hands. Nobody has yet designed an artificial hand which even comes close to replicating a human hand. Commercially available artificial hands typically have only the ability to open and close, with little other freedom of movement.

Generally, replacement hands and terminal devices are of two types: functional or cosmetic. The most frequently used cosmetic versions can neither open wide enough to hold many common objects nor flex tightly enough to hold small objects in a firm grip. This limits their functional range.

Functional hands are strong and sturdy mechanical hands, to which different types of terminal devices can be affixed. The terminal devices are designed so that one end of the terminal device fits easily into the small socket made in the prosthetic hand. The terminal devices are usually made of steel. A voluntary opening hook, which can be opened or closed whenever the user choses to do so, is one of the most commonly preferred terminal devices. Artisans, farmers and agricultural labourers can use these functional hands effectively for both farm and non-farm work, including ploughing the field, digging the ground, carpentry and welding.

The most commonly used hands are rigid hands and cosmetic hands. Presently, the most successful arrangement has been to operate the first and second fingers along with some motion of the thumb, in a three-jaw-chuck type of prehension pattern. Mechanical hands with finger phalange movement, which improves prehension, are also available in Asian and Pacific developing countries.

A manual worker will likely require a functional hand to replace even a non-dominant hand. For others, a cosmetic hand will likely be an adequate replacement, at least for a non-dominant hand. Unilateral amputees generally find it easier to learn to use their non-dominant hand than to use a functional prosthetic hand. Bilateral amputees are often best served by one functional hand with a hook as a terminal device and one cosmetic hand.

A hand prosthesis can be activated and operated either through body power or through an external power source (e.g., batteries). Myoelectric hands, operated through contact with electrodes in the socket, are popular in developed countries. They are used in a few countries in the region, including China, but their long-term usefulness has yet to be established and their cost is often high.

Currently, the only manufacturer of electronic hands in an Asian or Pacific developing country is the Nevedac Prosthetic Centre at Chandigarh, India. The Nevedac Centre's electronic hands, with switch-control systems, are made from indigenous materials. They are cheaper than myoelectric hands but just as effective. The Centre has also developed mechanical hands which allow all five fingers to move. People from afar have come to obtain these hands.

C. Orthoses

Orthoses are also known as calipers or braces. Although a brace is generally considered to be larger than a caliper, the two terms are often used interchangeably. This review uses only the more general term orthosis to avoid confusion.

Orthoses have two major purposes: first, to support or maintain a weak limb; and second, to help prevent or correct future deformities and contractures.

Only a few developing countries of the ESCAP region have paid substantial attention to the production of orthoses, in spite of large numbers requiring them. India has addressed the need for orthoses in response to the consequences of polio among many people. In those countries which produce orthoses, manufacturing capacities are not completely used.

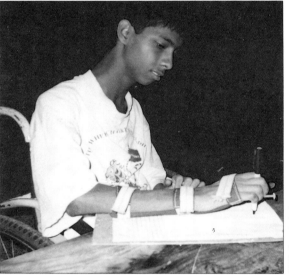

Writing splint (metal).

Knee-ankle-foot orthoses (KAFO).

A combination of hip knee ankle foot orthosis (HKAFO) and crutches has been used effectively by the Christian Medical College in Vellore, India, for rehabilitating paraplegic people in their own village surroundings (see Field Visit Notes in Madras Workshop Proceedings). Unlike most wheelchairs, this combination permits them to work in the field and thus remain productive members of their families, as well as allowing for regular exercise.

Metallic orthoses are the most common type of orthosis in developing

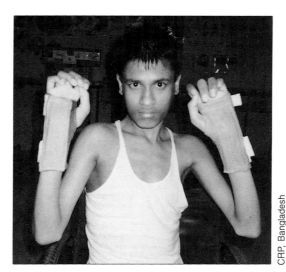

Wrist splint (metal).

CRP, Bangladesh

countries of the ESCAP region. Conventional metal lower-limb orthoses require the use of special shoes. These shoes are user-specific, so full orthoses can only be produced at a clinic or hospital with trained prosthetic and orthotic technicians. The special leather shoes required are made in the rehabilitation workshops to suit the size and condition of the user's foot. For example, the inside height of the shoe may have to be increased to account for limb shortening.

Unfortunately, many countries face a shortage of shoemakers. For this

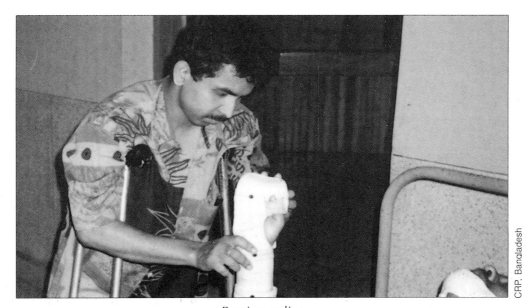

Resting splint.

CRP, Bangladesh

37

Feeding belt.

reason, India's rural programme attempted to use wooden clogs in place of leather shoes. However, these clogs were unstable, unattractive (because both feet and clogs became dirty quickly) and came loose after continuous use. As a result, users did not accept them.

Metal orthoses are heavy and prone to corrosion. The bracing often becomes excessive, disallowing the movement of muscles of the limb, which may have negative long-term consequences. Orthoses made of thermoplastic or polyvinyl chloride (PVC) are lighter. The most commonly used thermoplastic is polypropylene. A hybrid of plastic and metal is also used.[16]

For a child who needs a below-knee orthosis, a thermoplastic orthosis moulded to fit the child's leg and foot has these advantages:

(a) It weighs less and is often more comfortable than metal orthoses;

(b) It can fit the child comfortably and exactly (if made well);

(c) It is not prone to corrosion and can be worn easily with ordinary shoes.

---

16 See the Technical Specifications Supplement for information on the process of making orthoses.

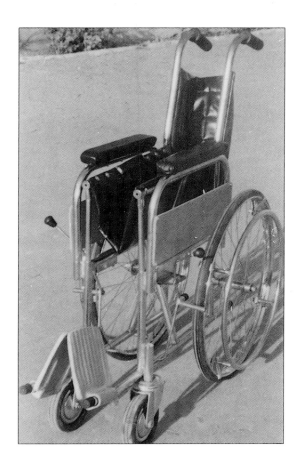

Nevedac wheelchair, folding model, with detachable sides, solid rubber tyres, fibreglass foot rests, padded arms rests, manually operated brakes and heavy duty castor wheels.

Price: Rs. 3,400/- (for Chandigarh)

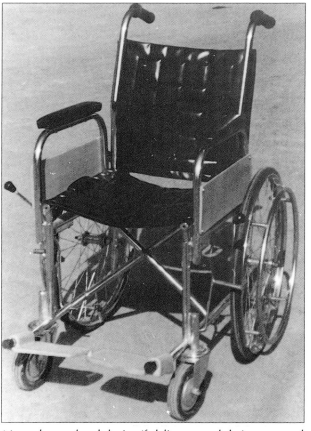

Nevedac wheelchair (folding model in normal position).

Nevedac tricycle (deluxe model): hand-propelled, chain-driven, with a fibreglass seat, handle bar, fitted with hand brake mechanism and a bell, pneumatic tyres and tubes and double chain driving arrangements, for operation with right or left hand. Price: Rs. 2,975/– (approxim., for Chandigarh). The Nevedac Centre, Chandigarh, India, also manufactures motorized (petrol-driven) tricycles, with heavy duty tyres/tubes, with different capacity (HP) engines. Their prices range between Rs. 20,000/– and Rs. 35,000/– each, for Chandigarh.

The fit of thermoplastic orthoses, however, is very close, and this often makes them feel uncomfortably hot in tropical climates. In addition, a casting must be made, which increases the complexity of the production process.

Even if a better design of thermoplastic orthosis existed, the limited availability of thermoplastics and the need for the related equipment would remain a deterrent to their use, especially in rural areas. Furthermore, thermoplastic orthoses are not yet produced in a modular way, so a rehabilitation centre will need in-house moulding facilities to produce them.

Finally, thermoplastic orthoses may not be suitable when, as a result of the type of disability faced, orthoses have to bear high loads and be very stable. In such cases, orthoses made of thermoplastic and metal may be the best option.

Source: All Nevedac items were contributed by Colonel D.S. Vohra, Director, Nevedac Prosthetic Centre, Chandigarh, India.

The hybrid of thermoplastic and metal will likely become the favoured material, as it has the advantages of both thermoplastic and metal. Such an orthosis is being prescribed in many places. However, it does require different machines, tools and technical skills in rehabilitation centres. It is easier for those centres to deal only with the technology required for one material.

The thermoplastics usually used for making orthoses are polypropylene and polyethylene. The strength of thermoplastic orthoses is insufficient to withstand the tough loading conditions imposed by the rough terrain and usage pattern in rural areas, such as when feet hit an obstacle and get bent in one direction. Glass-filled polypropylene has been used to overcome this problem, but it is expensive. Another solution is to include an aluminium support and aluminium knee joint in a polypropylene orthosis.

In India, for people with good biceps muscles and hand-on-knee gait, floor-reaction orthoses (FRO) have been found useful. An FRO is designed so that the toe strikes the ground first; the reaction force from the ground pushes back the knee, making it stable. As a result, users do not require a hand-on-knee gait. Some rehabilitation centres also use PVC pipes (which are used to carry water and are available locally) to produce orthoses.

D. Wheelchairs and ground mobility devices

Wheelchairs in developed countries often use high-technology materials like aluminium alloys, titanium and carbon fibre. The cost of such wheelchairs, however, is usually unaffordable by most users in Asian and Pacific developing countries. Non-availability of spare parts and maintenance facilities are additional drawbacks. As a result, steel is predominantly used for fabricating wheelchairs in the developing countries of the region. Aluminium alloys have recently been used for making wheelchairs in Thailand (see Box 6). These wheelchairs, however, are only suitable for movement on smooth surfaces.

NGOs in Cambodia use a wooden wheelchair (see Technical Specifications Supplement). Compared with metal

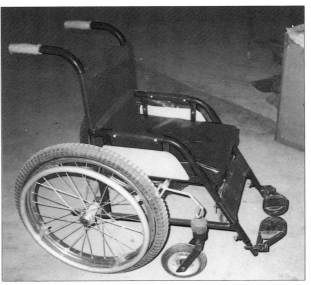

Child's wheelchair.

wheelchairs, wooden wheelchairs are stronger and easier to repair and adapt in rural areas. They were initially cheaper as well, although this advantage has faded with rises in the price of wood.

The design of wheelchairs used in Asian and Pacific developing countries has often been based on specifications intended for people in other regions of the world. These wheelchairs are often oversized. The width and depth of the seat and the height of the armrests are unsuitable for and unacceptable to their users.

Some wheelchairs in use in the region, especially those provided free of charge to users, were designed for use in institutions, especially hospitals – even though the actual use of the wheelchairs is in daily life. Such wheelchairs have many problems including:

(a) Inappropriate size;

(b) Difficulty of controlling the chairs;

(c) Poor facility for transferring in and out of the chairs;

(d) High cost;

(e) Unsuitability for rural use;

(f) Lack of durability;

(g) Difficulty and expense of repairs.

The utility of wheelchairs has been especially limited in rural areas. A study conducted in India, based on an analysis of 47 wheelchairs in use in 46 villages in different parts of the country, showed that many wheelchairs were used as push chairs, because the prescription was not correct or because the chairs were so designed that family members were inclined to push the chairs. Although wheelchairs could be useful outside the home, the smallness of houses made them practically useless indoors. Furthermore, rough terrain led to quick wear and tear and breakages, especially of the castor assembly, main wheel and brakes. The exposed metallic parts were corroded by moisture, dust, mud, and other substances common in those villages. Finally, stability and controllability were inadequate.[17]

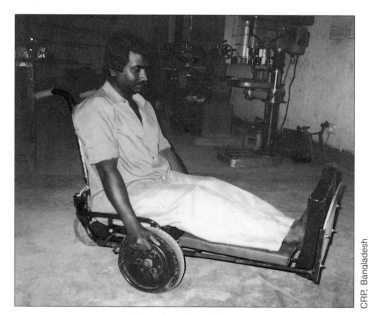

Low-level trolley.

CRP, Bangladesh

---

[17] R. Saha and others, "Study of Wheelchair Operations in Rural Areas Covered under the District Rehabilitation Centre (DRC) Scheme", *Indian Journal of Disability and Rehabilitation*, July-December 1990.

Cooking at ground level using a ground mobility device.

Jesuit Service Cambodia, an NGO, and the MacKean Rehabilitation Centre in Thailand, use a stronger castor wheel assembly, but feedback from users is not available. It is, however, clear that wheelchairs for use in rural areas have to be durable and sturdy. Wheelchairs for distribution to the rural poor must be redesigned to fit their lifestyles.

Most wheelchairs produced in the region have the conventional configuration of two castor wheels in the front and two main wheels in the back. An exception is a wheelchair made in Cambodia that has only one castor wheel in the front.

Ground mobility devices, or low wheelchairs, are similar to wheelchairs, but work at ground level rather than at chair level. They can be more useful than wheelchairs in places where many tasks are performed close to ground level, especially in rural areas. Such tasks include food preparation, welding, praying, eating, masonry and craft

work. The ground mobility device developed by the National Institute of Design in Ahmedabad, India, with contributions from the International Centre for the Advancement of Community Based Rehabilitation (ICACBR), was designed with the participation of women with disabilities and field tested by them. (See the Technical Specifications Supplement for descriptions of the parts and process required to produce the device.)

The Centre for the Rehabilitation of the Paralysed in Bangladesh has developed a similar ground-level trolley device.[18] The user sits on soft coconut fibre placed over an air-filled inner tube (from a scooter). The inner tube serves both as a cushion and as a toilet seat. A small removable pot fits into the metal frame of the trolley and is centred under the hole in the tube. The trolley is collapsible. Its back folds down and the projecting leg-rest slides in.

The production process for wheelchairs tends to be similar among most workshops, although the workshops and factories producing a large number of wheelchairs tend to involve more automation.[19]

18 David Werner, *Nothing about Us without us*, p. 194. HealthWrights, Palo Alto, U.S.A., 1998).

19 For information on the tools required to make wheelchairs, see Ralf Hotchkiss, *Independence through Mobility: A Guide to the Manufacture of the ATI-Hotchkiss wheelchair* Appropriate Technology International. Washington, DC,

Image credit (vertical): National Institute of Design, Ahmedabad, India

Trolley toilet: The tube functions as a cushion and toilet seat; a small pot fits into the metal frame of the trolley.

Back folds down; projecting leg-rest slides in.

Wheelchairs are mass-produced in a number of countries, including Bangladesh, Cambodia, China, India, Pakistan, Thailand and Viet Nam. In China, about 100,000 wheelchairs are produced per year. These are produced in 20 factories, some owned by the Government and some privately. Of these, ten produce wheelchairs solely for export.

In Cambodia and Malaysia, bilateral above-knee amputees have been provided wheelchairs in their workplaces. Many of these amputees are engaged in tailoring in vocational centres in Malaysia and in machine shops in Cambodia.

Armenia currently imports all its wheelchairs, but its Ministry of Social Welfare has begun a project to have wheelchairs, especially for children, made locally through the Yerevan Prosthetic Orthopedic Enterprise.

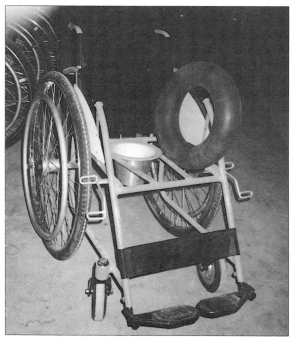

Wheelchair toilet with tube and pot.

BOX 8: THE WHEELCHAIR MAINTENANCE CLINIC, NONTHABURI, THAILAND

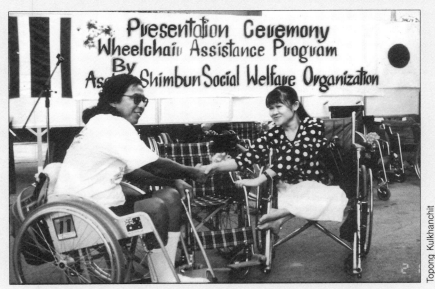

Wheelchair improvement, a new area for technical assistance.

Topong Kulkhanchit, as a wheelchair user himself and as President of the Association of the Physically Handicapped of Thailand (APHT), was dissatisfied with the standard institutional design of wheelchairs and the poor facilities available for their repair and maintenance. Mr. Topong and his friends decided to start a project to make new wheelchairs better suited for active lifestyles and to provide a proper maintenance service. Today, the Wheelchair Maintenance Clinic has an all-in-one programme covering the production, repair, and maintenance of wheelchairs, and training in all of these functions.

In 1991, Mr. Topong and his friends proposed such a project to the Asahi Shimbun Social Welfare Organization of Japan. Asahi Shimbun agreed to ship 100 renovated used wheelchairs from Japan to Thailand every year from 1993 to 1995, if the APHT would be responsible for customs procedures, local transportation, storage, distribution, and most importantly, maintenance. Since 1995, the APHT Wheelchair Maintenance Clinic has been able to develop and produce its own wheelchairs. Acting on a suggestion of Mr. Topong, Asahi Shimbun now ships wheelchairs to Bangladesh and the Philippines.

In 1993, the APHT sent two staff members (with disabilities) to Oita Taki Corporation in Japan for a month of training on wheelchair maintenance. In the following two years, these staff members were able to train many other local technicians. Some of those trainees now work at the Clinic. By 1996, the training became a TCDC programme, with people with disabilities from Bangladesh, the Philippines and Viet Nam joining its training course. In 1997, the trainees included two from Bangladesh, two from the Lao People's Democratic Republic, two from the Philippines, and three from Viet Nam, as well as 21 from Thailand. Every trainee builds at least one wheelchair during the course. Trainees acquire the skills to repair and maintain bicycles as well as wheelchairs.

The main Clinic in Nonthaburi sends most spare parts, free of charge, to provinces in Thailand where its trainees are working. This frees the provincial chapters of the Clinic from having to charge people in their communities. The Clinic operates 24 hours a day, seven days a week, with spare wheelchairs available on loan while regular wheelchairs are fixed.

E. Tricycles and adapted motorcycles

Many wheelchair manufacturers in developing countries of the ESCAP region also produce tricycles. Tricycles are devices with three main wheels; they are larger than wheelchairs but operated in similar ways (by hand, electricity or petrol). They are useful for long-distance mobility. In several developing countries of the region, tricycles have enabled people with disabilities to work far from their homes. A tricycle can also be used for carrying extra loads, such as groceries or household items. People in rural areas often prefer tricycles to wheelchairs because tricycles are sturdier and can more easily negotiate rough terrain.

Tricycles, however, have some drawbacks. A tricycle cannot replace a wheelchair for indoor and around-the-house mobility, as there will likely be insufficient space. Moreover, as tricycles are heavier than wheelchairs, users must have enough muscle power in their hands and upper bodies to propel manual tricycles.

For meeting different needs, many people with disabilities need both a wheelchair and a tricycle. In Cambodia, an attachment has been designed which makes it possible to convert a wheelchair into a tricycle. Jesuit Services Cambodia produces this attachment on a regular basis.

The most common configuration of tricycle is one wheel in the front used for steering and two main (rear) wheels which are attached to, and moved by, a chain or a hand lever.

BOX 9: WHEELCHAIR TCDC OUTCOME IN THE PHILIPPINES

Following their training at the Wheelchair Maintenance Clinic, Thailand, and further short-term training in Japan, a small wheelchair workshop was set up in Cebu City, Philippines, by one of the Filipino participants.

Four wheelchair users are employed at the workshop run by an organization of persons with disabilities, Handicapped's Anchor is Christ (HACI), Inc. Two of the workers had been trained in welding in the National Manpower and Youth Council, Cebu City. HACI had negotiated for their admission to the welding course. It had also mobilized funding for their training materials, as well as for subsidies for their daily transport and food.

A donation of equipment amounting to US$2,000 enabled the HACI workshop to commence production, using a Japanese wheelchair design.

Similar wheelchair workshops run by persons with disabilities also exist in Bacolod, Davao and Manila.

The HACI workshop is just one year in existence. It produces three types of wheelchair: stainless steel (Pesos 11,000), chrome-plated (Pesos 9,000) and painted (8,000). The castor wheels are imported from Taiwan Province of China. Seven wheelchairs are produced each month.

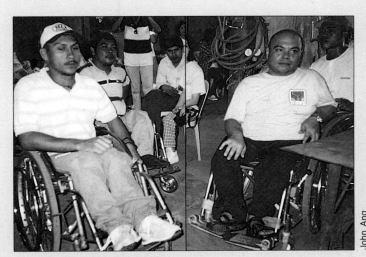

HACI's four wheelchair user workers.

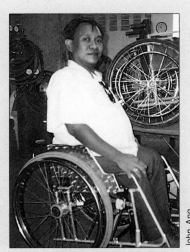

Mr. Rolando Boy Tirol, President, HACI, trained in Thailand and Japan.

The Shanghai Wheelchair Factory makes the best-selling manual tricycles in China, at market prices between US$70 and US$140. Three models, in different sizes, are driven with only one hand; the other hand is for direction control. A fourth model, the SJ26Q, can be driven by two hands or two feet. When two hands drive it, they also control direction. Although minor repair of these tricycles can be performed at bicycle repair sites, some parts can only be obtained from the manufacturers, which makes major repair difficult and inconvenient.

A wheelchair converted into a tricycle.

R. Saha

It is also possible to produce a petrol-driven motorized tricycle similar to a motorcycle. About 20,000 motorized tricycles are produced in China each year. The market prices for such a motorized tricycle are between about US$410 and US$720. The most popular model is Model CJ50ZC manufactured by Chongqing Jialing Industry Co. Ltd.

A motorcycle modified and adapted to fit the needs of wheelchair users can be an important assistive device which provides users with mobility over long as well as short distances. The cost of such a device is, however, high. Furthermore, in some cases, government action has hindered more than helped their production. Not only is such adaptation rarely if ever subsidized, but in some countries, including Thailand, it is actually illegal to produce and drive an adapted motorcycle. This illustrates the importance of flexible regulations and the problems of imposing legal sanctions for violating quality-control standards and procedures.

An Indian hand-operated tricycle.

Serm Plao model with new shaft added. It was innovated in Samut Prakarn, Thailand, by a wheelchair user – member of the Association of Prapadaeng Disabled People.

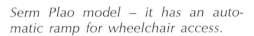

Serm Plao model – it has an automatic ramp for wheelchair access.

Puang Khang model – an innovation by a wheelchair user and member of the Chiang Mai Club of Disabled Persons. This model, unlike the Serm Plao, has no new shaft attached to it; instead there is more space on the side.

Source: All items on this page were contributed by Colonel Topong Kulkhanchit, APHT, Thailand.

Post-polio mechanic sitting on a floor-level trolley to adapt a motorbike into the Serm Plao model.

Motorized tricycles adapted by the Wheelchair Maintenance Clinic, Nonthaburi, Thailand.

In Thailand, there are two popular designs of this adaptation. The first places a bay at the side of the motorcycle onto which a wheelchair can be ridden, facing forward. The handlebars are moved to the wheelchair user's focal point and the transmission, normally operated by foot pedal, is operated with a lever. This modification costs 6,000-7,000 baht,[20] in addition to the cost of the motorcycle.

The second modification, known as the *Seum Plao*, produces a result similar to the Chinese design for a motorized tricycle. The user sits in the middle of the vehicle, which makes the

Bangladeshi adaptation of the motorized three-wheeler.

modification stronger, safer, and more stable. However, this design requires a modification of the cylinder, which is difficult and involves more sophisticated mechanical skills. As a result, the cost of the modification is about 12,000 baht (US$330).

---

[20] Equivalent to approximately US$150-200 in September 1997.

F. Devices for people with visual impairments

Most devices for blind people are not highly user-specific. It is therefore easier to mass-produce devices for blind people than most devices for people with locomotor disabilities. Nevertheless, decentralized production has the advan-tage of facilitating distribution. The ease of decentralized distribution and the (potentially) lower costs of mass produc-tion should be carefully weighed while deciding on a production strategy.

Devices for people with visual im-pairments range from simple mechanical tools to sophisticated computerized de-vices. Most Asian and Pacific developing countries do not produce devices like

---

BOX 10: MAKING USE OF LOW VISION

People with low vision are often treated as blind, for a number of reasons. The first problem is a lack of knowledge and understanding about low vision. Second is a lack of appropriate low-vision training. The third problem is a lack of assistive devices. Assistive devices can aid some of these "blind" people to make effective use of the residual vision they have, so that they can, for example, read ordinary writ-ing rather than braille. Unfor-tunately, the limited availability of optical magnifying compo-nents, such as lenses, means that large numbers of people in Asian and Pacific developing countries remain handicapped.

WHO data estimates that one per cent of people in In-dia, 0.6 per cent in China, and 0.8 per cent in the rest of the Asia-Pacific region were blind in 1990, a total of about 21.4 million. The estimate of people with low vision, by contrast, is about 1.9 per cent.

Assistive devices can make possible the effective use of residual vision.

white canes and braille slates despite the simplicity of such devices.

Speech synthesizers are an important device for the education and employment of people with visual impairments. Most speech synthesizers currently in use are available only in English. Speech synthesizers have been produced in India using speech chips available from Japan, Taiwan Province of China, and the United States of America. Such chips are expensive, however, and a more recent policy is to use special software developed for use with the sound blaster-compatible sound cards readily available in the market.

Thailand has developed a package for optical character recognition of the Thai language. This will likely empower many people with visual disabilities to access better educational and employment opportunities.

Many countries import their mechanical braillers, braille shorthand machines and computerized braille embossers from developed countries. Braillers have been produced in India for many years. China now makes braillers and all their parts locally.

Close circuit TV system.

Low-speed computerized braille embossers based on indigenous designs and locally available parts are now produced in India. These embossers are useful in classrooms and other situations where the workload is not heavy. Prices of these locally produced embossers are lower than the prices of similar imported devices. Closed-circuit television systems with magnifying facilities are also produced in India.

Thermoplastic braille writing frames are produced in China, India and Thailand. The frames made in China and Thailand are four-line frames, i.e., the frame has to be moved after each four lines that the user writes.

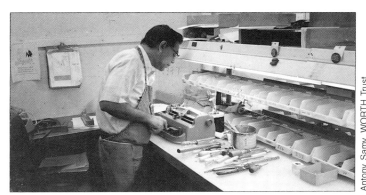

Making the Worth Perkins brailler at WORTH Trust.

Braille frames can save on consumption of braille paper if they can also perform interpointing writing, i.e., braille writing which uses the space between two dots for writing on the reverse side of a page, allowing both sides of the page to be used. A 26-line interpointing writing frame developed in India is now produced there on a regular basis. This is made from locally available plastic material.

To produce braillers and braille writing frames in large numbers, accurate dies must be designed and produced so that the devices can be produced using an injection-moulding process. Metallic devices are generally being replaced with plastic ones because of the tremendous saving

Braillers are useful, but the long-term challenge is to ensure equal access to computer technology, especially to break gender- and disability-stereotyping.

in weight, and because of increasing availability of good injection-moulding facilities for making the plastic parts. Forging and machining are essential for metallic parts, such as levers and keys used in braillers or facilities for casting.

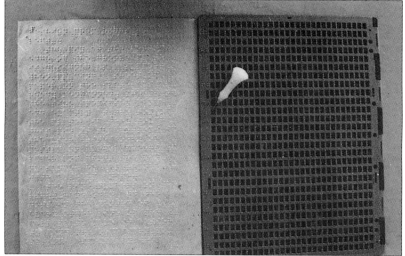

The Indian braille interpointing writing frame.

Rehabilitation Technology, Centre Ministry of Welfare, Government of India

G. Devices for people with hearing impairments

Few developing countries in the ESCAP region produce hearing aids. The exceptions are China and India, both of which produce many types of hearing aids. China has set up joint ventures with foreign companies for the production of hearing aids. In India, on the other hand, all the companies making hearing aids are domestic ones. The hearing aids are produced according to Indian standards, which are similar to international standards.

Producers of hearing aids generally do not produce their own parts, but obtain them from other sources. The production techniques, which are similar to those used to produce electronic audio systems, require trained engineers and technicians.

Many useful devices other than hearing aids are neither produced nor imported by most Asian and Pacific developing countries. These include group hearing aids, telephone amplifiers, inductive couplers, vibrating indicators, TV listening devices, telephones with flashing lights, vibrating alarm clocks, FM hearing aids and loop induction systems.

David Werner

CHAPTER IV

DESIGN AND PRODUCTION OF PARTS

The success of a production strategy for finished assistive devices inevitably depends on the availability of their parts. Some parts, such as castor wheels in wheelchairs, are subsystems, i.e., they act as one unit, but contain other parts within them. Many parts useful in the production of assistive devices (e.g., ball bearings and wheelchair tyres) are already produced in developing countries of the ESCAP region for incorporation in other domestic products such as bicycles.

A. Prostheses

Many countries, including Bhutan, Fiji, Malaysia, Maldives, Nepal, Sri Lanka and Thailand, import parts for prostheses from within and outside of the region.

A strong system of local production of parts for prostheses now exists in several developing countries of the ESCAP region.

Cambodia's well-developed system for producing prosthesis parts is based on the assistance of international NGOs providing rehabilitation services. In Cambodia, most parts for lower-limb and upper-limb prostheses are manufactured by one international NGO, the International Committee of the Red Cross (ICRC). The parts are made of polypropylene (sometimes recycled), aluminium and steel. Most raw material is imported. The production is carried out in a factory with modern facilities for vacuum forming, injection moulding, welding, stamping and milling.

The parts used were designed at the ICRC Headquarters in Geneva, Switzerland, which produces, according to its international specifications, the dies and moulds used in Cambodia. There are now attempts to have the dies made locally. In the past few years, the factory has adopted a more uniform production process, substantially reducing the production cost and time.

In India, most parts for prostheses are manufactured by a government-owned factory, Artificial Limb Manufacturing Corporation (ALIMCO). ALIMCO was set up in the 1970s using foreign technology and knowledge, but today the company is totally self-reliant. This self-reliance has been achieved by recruiting qualified local engineers to manage the industry. ALIMCO has also developed new methods of production and quality control.

China uses a variety of strategies for the production of prosthesis parts. It produces most parts locally, but also imports some high-technology parts, such as high-performance prosthetic feet. China produces about 50,000 foot pieces made of rubber and wood in three Government-owned factories.

The knee system of an AK prosthesis is the part that most distinguishes producing an AK prosthesis from producing a BK prosthesis. The knee system includes the artificial knee and the mechanism that links it to the shank; the knee, in turn, includes the knee joint and its enclosure.

BOX 11: DR. P.K. SETHI AND THE JAIPUR DESIGNS

R. Saha

Dr. P.K. Sethi

Dr. P.K. Sethi is one of the inventors of the Jaipur prosthesis and its component, the Jaipur Foot. Dr. Sethi first thought of the idea for these devices in 1965, when he was prescribing solid-ankle-cushion-heel (SACH) feet to people with amputated lower limbs in Jaipur, India. He would ask users, in casual encounters outside the hospital setting, how satisfied they were with their new feet – and found that many of them had returned to using crutches instead.

The production team had not realized that the SACH Foot, intended to be worn with shoes for sitting in chairs, was not suitable for Indians who walked barefoot and sat on the floor. By 1970, with the help of his fellow device producers, Dr. Sethi had the new designs which have since become known as the Jaipur prosthesis and Jaipur Foot.

As well as their cultural appropriateness, these devices have two other features that led to their popularity. First, they can be made easily by local artisans with local materials, so that once the design is known, they can be produced anywhere, not just in hospitals or other centres with specialized equipment and expertise. Second, Dr. Sethi's team did not patent the designs, making them available free of charge and thus reducing the cost to users. As a result, the devices have proved useful not only in the ESCAP region, but also in Africa, and Latin America.

Going about barefoot is still the norm in many developing countries of the region.

The knee system is crucial for an AK prosthesis user, as it determines the types of activities that she or he can undertake. Daily life in many countries and areas of the ESCAP region involves ground-level activities such as food preparation, washing, eating, praying, welding, masonry and craft work. A knee system must therefore allow for rotation of the limb and flexing of the foot in a way that permits sitting and squatting on the ground.

To provide a normal appearance during walking, the knee joint should not buckle as the amputee rolls over the artificial foot during the stance phase of walking. This is achieved by using mechanical friction around a bolt that connects the socket to the thigh. The bolt is located behind the path of the weight of the body so that it will not buckle when the user is standing straight.

The single-axis joint, so named because it can move around only one axis, is the most commonly used knee joint because of its simplicity and low cost. One of the joint's limitations is that its appearance is normal during walking at only one walking speed. Its users must be careful while walking, especially on uneven ground, to avoid stumbling. Other types of joints exist, such as the polycentric knee joint, but they are expensive and difficult to repair and maintain. As a result, they are not widely used in the region.

The knee joint HI2B is a good example of a part produced with a simple but professional technique. Handicap International (HI), an NGO, produces it in cooperation with the Sirindhorn National Medical Rehabilitation Centre in Thailand. Made of PVC, this joint can be produced for less than 200 baht[20] (approximately US$5.50) and requires less than a day for a technician to be trained to produce it, but it is of high enough quality to last at least a year.

Participants in a 1995 international conference in Phnom Penh on prosthetic technology observed that the most common failures in lower-limb prosthesis components are the following:

---

20 Equivalent to approximately US$5.50 in September 1997.

- Foot separation of the keel from the foot body; cracks, splits, and tears in the foam/latex; failure of the foot-ankle attachment.

- Knee extension stop wear/failure; bushing wear at the joint axis; cracks on and around the knee axis; wood degradation secondary to infestation, fungus, rot (this may also happen with glass-reinforced thermoplastic); failure of socket-knee interface.

- Socket material fatigue and stress fracture.

The participants concluded that a desirable overall life span for the knee of a prosthesis was two to three years. For the foot, they concluded that one and a half to two years would be acceptable.[21] To make the foot more durable than this would significantly increase its weight.

Prosthetic feet

Imported prosthetic feet have been found deficient in Asian and Pacific developing countries for three reasons. First is the exorbitant cost of importing prosthetic feet from developed countries. Second, many imported feet have not been suitable for use in local cultural environments. Third, the imported feet are often not durable, especially under the rugged physical conditions in rural areas.

Most people in rural areas need to walk barefoot, work in fields, squat, sit on the ground and engage in manual tasks. They need a durable foot, preferably one that can last for significantly longer than a year under such conditions. Prosthetic feet currently being produced do not satisfy this requirement. Getting a new foot fitted annually may be a major disruption in the lives of some users, and may simply be impossible for others.

The solid-ankle-cushion-heel (SACH) foot is commonly used in the region, but it is not suitable for barefoot walking. It is also covered in polyurethane foam, which does not stay intact in hot climates.

A technician (wearing a below-knee Jaipur prosthesis) reinforcing the rubber in the Jaipur Foot mould before vulcanization.

---

21 Report of Syndicate D9.5, in report of ISPO (International Society for Prosthetics and Orthotics) Consensus Conference on Appropriate Prosthetic Technology for Developing Countries, held in Phnom Penh, 5-10 June 1995.

BOX 12: PARTS FOR DIFFERENT LOWER-LIMB ORTHOSES

Type of orthosis	Abbrev.	Compensates for	Parts used
Hip Knee Ankle Foot Orthosis	HKAFO	Weakness and deformities in the hips and legs	Pelvic band, hip joint with lock, tuber band, thigh band, knee-joint bar assembly, knee joint, knee cap, calf band, ankle bar assembly, ankle joint, stirrup, footwear.
Knee Ankle Foot Orthosis	KAFO	Weakness in the portion of leg above the knee, the knee itself, the ankle and the foot	Tuber band, knee joint with lock, calf band, knee-joint bar assembly, ankle bar assembly, ankle joint, stirrup, insole, modified shoes.
Ankle Foot Orthosis	AFO	Weakness or deformities in the ankle, foot and the portion of leg below the knee	Calf band, ankle bar assembly, ankle joint, stirrup, insole, modified shoes.
Foot Orthosis	None	Deformities in the foot	Insole, modified shoes.

The Mahavir Viklang Sahayta Samiti, an NGO based in Jaipur, India, developed the Jaipur Foot as a possible substitute for the SACH Foot. The Jaipur Foot is made of latex and microcellular (sponge) rubber (see the Technical Specifications Supplement for details of its production.) It is cheaper than the SACH Foot and well suited for squatting, cross-legged sitting, barefoot walking and even climbing trees. It is, however, heavier than the SACH Foot and designed primarily for use in an aluminium prosthesis. Furthermore, since all the steps in its production are manual, quality may vary from foot to foot.

Countries currently using Jaipur Feet include India and Sri Lanka. Most countries produce SACH Feet using the technique employed in making the Jaipur Foot (although some do not vulcanize the Foot).

59

Most NGOs in Cambodia use a rubber SACH Foot designed by Handicap International (HI). HI identified a privately-owned factory in Phnom Penh, which makes bicycle-wheel inner tubes and other rubber items. This factory now produces this Foot in large numbers. Another factory, which specializes in making plastic boilers for drinking water, produces the keel out of polypropylene with an injection machine.

The materials for the Foot are locally available. Polypropylene is recycled from prostheses and natural rubber comes from the Cambodian province of Kompong Cham. HI provided the technical support to both factories by transferring the relevant knowledge and supplying moulds, presses and a few other machines. Both these factories are likely to continue to meet the needs of Cambodians without further technical support from HI.

The Cambodian-made Foot pieces are also exported to the Lao People's Democratic Republic, Thailand and Viet Nam. The same design of Foot is now produced in Africa. The Government of Viet Nam plans to start the production of this Foot in Viet Nam in association with HI.

B. Orthoses

In some developing countries of the ESCAP region, the number of people with conditions that result in a need for orthoses (such as post-polio paralysis) is diminishing. In others, the number of people requiring orthoses is comparable to the number requiring

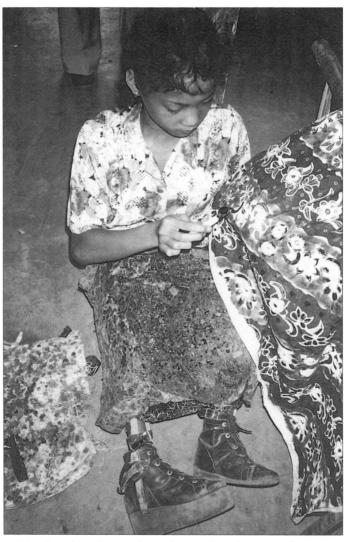

Wearing locally-made orthopaedic shoes, Indonesia.

prostheses. In both types of countries, however, parts for prostheses are more commonly produced than those for orthoses. There are, however, indications that the production of orthoses is increasing.

Many parts for orthoses can be made in workshops, but only in relatively limited quantities. Producing the parts in large numbers could achieve economies of scale, ensure uniform quality of parts and enable rehabilitation centres to produce orthoses in a shorter time than is presently the case. In India, parts are produced by the Artificial Limb Manufacturing Company (ALIMCO), a government corporation. They are distributed all over the country, as well as exported to neighbouring countries.

C. Wheelchairs and tricycles

Wheelchair production in many developing countries of the ESCAP region would be more cost-effective if it could take advantage of economies of scale already existing in the bicycle industry. This can be achieved by using standard bicycle parts, such as bicycle wheels, tyres and spokes, in the production of wheelchairs. The cost and production time required to obtain parts this way is considerably less than the cost of producing them specifically for wheelchairs.

Countries with a strong bicycle industry are thus better equipped to produce wheelchairs.

Tricycle manufacturers tend to buy most parts (usually bicycle parts) from outside rather than producing them in-house.

D. Devices for people with visual impairments

Assistive devices for people with visual impairments are not produced in many developing countries of the ESCAP region. Production of related parts, whether optical, electronic, electromagnetic or mechanical, is also limited, but some progress has been made. For example, speech synthesizers and optical character recognition packages in local languages have been produced in India and Thailand. The production of aspheric lenses, which can magnify images by more than five times without distortion, is being considered in India.

Braillers may require special spare parts to keep them in working order. Countries which make braillers are producing these parts. Their domestic production facilitates local maintenance and technical support for the devices.

E. Devices for people with hearing impairments

Assistive devices for people with hearing impairments make extensive use of electronic parts, which only a few developing countries of the ESCAP region can produce. Most developing countries in the region lack personnel with the necessary skills and expertise. Furthermore, batteries are a crucial part of many devices for people with hearing impairments. Most developing countries in the region import batteries although they are produced in the region. A similar situation exists concerning the production of the diagnostic equipment needed for the assessment of hearing loss.

Many parts, including transistors, simple integrated circuits, plastic cords, switches and connectors, are produced in China and India. However, receivers, microphones and special integrated circuits have to be imported even by those countries. Most of the listed parts have many applications and are not meant exclusively for use in equipment for people with hearing impairments.

Wang Tao (a motor-tricycle user), CDPF

Chinese motor-tricycle

Brand: Jia Ling; type: CJ50ZC; price: RMB 3,980 Yuan (about US$ 480) – domestic retail price in China. For a motor-tricycle with electronic starter (ignition lock/electronic ignitor/key ignitor) an extra charge of RMB 700 Yuan (about US$ 84.3) is added to the ordinary price.

CHAPTER V

ISSUES IN INDIGENOUS PRODUCTION

The term "indigenous production" is used in the broadest sense in this publication. It refers to the use of local, indigenous knowledge, skills, and methods of production. The most important criterion for production to be considered indigenous is that the production process has been thoroughly assimilated into local conditions by the local people on a sustainable basis.

The choice of a strategy for the production of assistive devices will vary considerably from country to country. Every country will need to consider:

(a) Economic, social and political priorities;

(b) Availability of personnel, infrastructure, raw materials, parts and funds;

(c) Cost of locally produced devices, compared with the cost of importing devices;

(d) User demand.

In addition to factory-based and other conventional forms of production, the informal sector also produces assistive devices in a decentralized way, often in rural areas. Specific needs motivate families, helpers of people with disabilities and other community members to produce devices with whatever materials and production techniques are available to them. User-specific devices are sometimes produced at workshops for vehicle maintenance and repair. In most cases, they are produced in rehabilitation centres run by Governments, NGOs, hospitals and colleges.

A. User-specific devices

A central issue in production, so far generally neglected, is the extent to which devices are user-specific. An orthosis must be fitted to the size of a user's leg, not simply taken off a shelf. At minimum, a workshop must take specific measurements of the shape of the affected leg and the location or height of various joints.

Although a wheelchair does not require the same degree of precise measurement, it must also be considered a highly user-specific device. Making wheelchairs in one "universal" extra-large size makes no more sense than making clothes in one extra-large size. People are of different sizes, and will therefore require different-sized wheelchairs. This is a problem of particular concern in the Asia-Pacific region, as wheelchairs imported from other regions (often through donations) and designed to fit people in those regions are often too large for local people.

Just like clothes, wheelchairs can still be used if they are the wrong size – but they will be uncomfortable and awkward. For children, this could adversely affect their growth and development. Producing "one-size-fits-all" wheelchairs may be useful when a wheelchair is to be used only under special conditions, as in a hospital, or on a very short-term basis, as for a wheelchair temporarily loaned to a user whose regular wheelchair is being repaired. But it would be wrong to assume that such wheelchairs are suitable for long-term, daily use.

B. Appropriate technologies and production methods

International NGOs have made valuable contributions to the initiation and upgrading of the production and distribution of assistive devices in developing countries of the ESCAP region. In some cases, however, the level of technology introduced may be too complex for the countries' current level of infrastructure and support services. In some places, local expertise could not be developed on time to fully utilize the presence of such NGOs.

Devices appropriate for the environment of a developing country often use a simpler, less sophisticated technology than the devices adopted in developed countries. Unfortunately, this often leads them to be regarded as inferior, even if their usefulness, durability and ease of repair could make them superior under local conditions.

However, poor methods of production can sometimes result in bad experiences with appropriate technology, which leads people to mistrust appropriately produced devices. The devices produced and the methods of producing them must be at both an appropriate level of technology and a high level of technique: simple, but professional.

Not every device produced within a country's boundaries is necessarily appropriate for use in that country. Some developing countries in the ESCAP region have imported for local use techniques invented in developed countries, without major effort to adapt that knowledge to local user needs. Long-term dependency on foreign expertise in the production of devices and in the import of parts and materials, especially from developed countries, can make devices thus produced much less appropriate for local conditions. NGOs need to take care to ensure that the beneficiaries of their programmes will not be left stranded if the supply of foreign technicians' skills ends.

C. Mass production

Mass production of assistive devices and their parts may help reduce their costs through economies of scale. It may also reduce the time required for production. There is, however, a corresponding increase in the cost and time for distribution, although mass production does allow a wider distribution network to be set up.

In many cases, however, mass production of assistive devices is impossible or undesirable, because it generally requires finished products to be almost identical. Although wheelchairs can be mass-produced, for example, they must still fit the requirements of each individual user. For further discussion see section A on "User-Specific devices" in this Chapter.

Theoretically, devices may be produced using new flexible "just-in-time" methods that would allow them to achieve the economies of scale found in a factory while still being responsive to user requirements. In practice, however, the state of local infrastructure in developing countries makes this difficult. The difficulty is exaggerated by a view, commonly held among producers, that assistive devices are not profitable. Such a system of production might be desirable as a future goal, but at present, it generally makes much more sense for developing countries to decentralize their production systems.

Mass production is most useful for those devices (e.g., vibrating alarm clocks) which do not have

For a child's growth, the proper size and fit of a device are all-important.

to fit a particular set of body measurements. For devices which are user-specific to even a small degree, a decentralized system of production makes it easier for people with disabilities to approach production sites to specify their requirements.

The advantages of mass production could also be realized for some user-specific devices if the mass-produced devices were adjustable. For example, some wheelchairs with adjustable height, footrest position and width are now available.

Even when the finished devices must or should be custom-built, mass production of parts can still reduce costs through economies of scale. Where possible, mass production of parts makes finished devices cheaper, quicker to produce, more easily available, and easier to repair. Producing parts through a machine reduces their variability, thus there is greater assurance of uniform quality.

However, a system of mass production of parts combined with decentralized production of finished devices must be

65

supported by solid distribution networks in order to transport the parts to the production centres. It also requires a considerable investment of capital.

In China and India, there is surplus capacity in some factories producing parts and finished assistive devices.

D. Prescription

Every assistive device must be appropriate for the person who uses it. Even the least user-specific devices, like braillers or vibrating alarm clocks, may not fit well with a user's lifestyle. People who prescribe assistive devices, whether

---

Box 13: Assessment: Key Questions

(a) How old are you?

(b) Do you live alone or with others? If the respondent lives with others, ask: In what ways might they be helpful or a problem?

(c) What is your occupation?

(d) How far is your house from this workshop? If the distance is more than is convenient for the respondent, ask: How did you get here? Do you plan to go back today? If not, how will you manage overnight accommodation?

(e) What disability are you looking for help with?

(f) What caused it? How old were you when this happened?

(g) Have you had an assistive device before? If the answer is yes, ask: When did you get it and how long did you have it? What were the good and bad aspects of wearing it? Who prescribed it for you?

(h) What do you expect a new assistive device will be like?

(i) What do you want to be able to do with it?

The last two questions are especially important. Some potential users may have heard about the availability of assistive devices without knowing how they can personally benefit from one. Others may want a device which is inappropriate for their situation. They may want a motorized wheelchair after seeing one on television, for example, without having considered the resources required for maintaining it.

Source: Mr. Yann Drouet, Prosthetics and Orthotics Expert, Handicap International – Thailand.

doctors, technicians or community-based rehabilitation (CBR) workers, should ask questions of prospective users about their lives, to optimize the chances that the potential users will receive the best devices for their own situations. See Box 13 for a sample list of such questions.

When rehabilitation personnel prescribe devices, it is helpful for them to be able to specify what kind of device is needed. At present, many rehabilitation personnel tend to offer general prescriptions, such as "this person needs a prosthesis", rather than being able to give a specific description helpful for technicians, such as "this person needs an above-knee prosthesis for the lower limb, section socket, tubular system, knee XXXX with brake, and foot 1D10 (dynamic)". A general prescription may result in a device that is unsuitable for the user (e.g., it is too short or too heavy).

This situation is common where rehabilitation personnel know little about assistive devices. There is an unfortunate gap between doctors and other health workers, who know little about assistive devices, and technicians, who know little about the medical or anatomical aspects of disabilities. If the two groups could work more closely with one another and learn something about each other's work, they would be better able to meet user needs.

Prescription must take into account the availability of support services for repair and maintenance, in the long and short term. A device which cannot easily be repaired or maintained is not a good or useful device.

In conditions of poverty in the developing countries of the region, it is unreasonable for prescribers to expect adherence to the strict standards for medical procedures common in developed countries. For example, prosthetists trained in developed countries sometimes have low regard for procedures of amputation surgery in developing countries. It is often said that such surgery is "improperly" performed, as it may lead to scarred stumps or stumps of a non-optimal size. But it is naive to expect that most rural areas will have access to the facilities or skills to perform "proper" amputation surgery and make the subsequent fitting of artificial limbs easier, when many such areas do not even have primary health care services.

It is indeed regrettable that amputation surgery cannot always be performed precisely with a view to fitting a new prosthetic limb. However, at least currently, it is not feasible to change this situation. In the meantime, it is more practical to adapt to the situation. Prosthetists need to accept that most emergency surgery will likely lead to stumps that are not the most optimal for fitting artificial limbs. Furthermore, they need to accept the reluctance of many amputees to undergo a second surgery to mend the stump to a more "acceptable" shape and size. Instead, Asian and Pacific developing countries must develop and use prostheses that can adapt to non-standard amputation procedures.

E. Quality control

In many developing countries of the ESCAP region, interest has recently increased in ensuring the quality of devices produced domestically. Some, including India and Viet Nam, have started to formulate quality-control standards for assistive devices, often similar to those of the International Standards Organization (ISO).

Rushing to adopt such standards is rarely advisable, however. The primary need in developing countries of the region is to produce assistive devices in large enough quantities that everyone who needs a device can get one. High standards may raise production costs (costs that will be passed on to users or to Governments and NGOs). They may also discourage innovation of new products. People often face a choice between a device that does not meet ISO-type standards and no device at all.

This caveat does not preclude the formation of some system of quality control, provided that any such system carefully takes into account local needs and conditions, and that users play a central role in its design. Simply copying a list of standards adopted by developed countries will likely have undesirable consequences.

It is reasonable for a Government to expect a certain level of quality in the devices it provides free of charge to the poor. But this level of quality should be ensured only through withholding of funding, not through legal sanctions. For the Government to impose fines (or more severe penalties) on those who produce devices that do not meet the standards adopted would be an undesirable restraint on innovation, which could hurt more than help people with disabilities. Standards and restrictions which make it illegal to produce adapted motorcycles significantly decrease the mobility of people with disabilities.

The term "quality" should include technique as well as technology. Quality control should ensure that, for example, technicians make devices in exactly the right size for their users and align them properly, as well as requiring durable materials and parts.

High quality alone does not make a device right for its user. The ultimate measure of an assistive device is long-term user satisfaction. A wheelchair produced for a farmer may be of high quality in terms of good technique, the right technology and external appearance, but if the farmer can only do her job with crutches rather than a wheelchair, the "high-quality" device is not a good one for her.

An appropriate system of quality control for assistive devices in a developing country of the ESCAP region will have the following features:

(a) Be technically feasible and practical in the environments of the majority of users;

(b) Not contribute to an increase in the cost of devices beyond acceptable limits, in either the short or the long term;

(c) Not restrict the further development of products;

(d) Not specify that all devices must have characteristics which most devices currently in use do not already have.

F. NGO-government cooperation

There are many fine examples in the Asia-Pacific region of cooperation between Governments and NGOs in the provision of assistive devices. NGOs have played an active role, with government support, in developing local capacity for the production of assistive devices. Governments often provide the funding, equipment or infrastructure needed for specific NGO-initiated projects. They also help select sites for NGO projects to ensure their sustainability. Governments are also able to support NGO efforts by coordinating diverse agencies to enhance production and distribution. Effective coordination can lead to better dialogue and exchange of information among people in different parts of a country who may be engaged in similar efforts in production or design, including community members and local workshop technicians.

In many cases, NGOs fund small pilot projects and provide technical assistance, often in the form of specialized expertise.

In many Asian and Pacific developing countries, the trend until recently has been for NGOs engaged in rehabilitation to operate only in major cities and their suburbs, without a presence in rural areas. This problem is increasingly being addressed, not least by changes in funding criteria to encourage NGO action in the rural areas and increase rehabilitation services in support of rural communities.

Wearing a below-knee polypropylene (PP) prosthesis made in a community workshop.

G. Raw materials

Raw materials commonly used in Asian and Pacific developing countries for various types of assistive devices include:

(a) Aluminium, in the form of tubes and strips (for wheelchairs, white canes and orthoses);

(b) Steel, in the form of tubes and strips (e.g., for wheelchairs, knee joints, walkers and orthoses);

(c) Titanium (for prostheses and wheelchairs);

(d) Wood (for wheelchairs, prostheses and crutches);

(e) Thermoplastics of different types, such as polypropylene (for prosthetic sockets);

(f) Polyester resin (for sockets);

(g) Epoxy and polyurethane (for prosthetic feet);

(h) Polymethyl methylacrylate (for lenses of devices for people with low vision);

(i) Polyvinyl chloride (PVC) (for orthoses);

(j) Nylon, polyethylene (for prostheses and orthoses);

(k) Natural rubber (for prosthetic feet);

(l) Glass fibre (for orthoses);

(m) Carbon fibre (for prostheses, wheelchairs);

(n) Leather (for shoes, prostheses, orthoses);

(o) Different types of solvents and catalysts, canvas, cloth and plaster of Paris (POP).

Some countries have chosen to use only indigenously available raw materials. The advantages of this approach are that it is more likely to lead to the development of local capabilities, it is often lower in cost, and there is greater assurance of the supply of the materials. Imports of raw materials and parts, especially from developed countries, can create a level of dependency on foreign expertise and technologies that may prove expensive and unsustainable in the long term.

The disadvantage of this approach is that more effective or efficient materials cannot be used. This means that the devices may be lower in quality, higher in cost, or both. For example, aluminium and its alloys substantially reduce the weight of many devices, but these materials are not available in many developing countries of the ESCAP region. For this reason, there is a general tendency to import at least some raw materials.

Recycling available material is one way to obtain useful raw materials cheaply. Factories in Indonesia and Viet Nam recycle scrap metal from aeroplanes and helicopters into parts for orthoses. Parts of old prostheses are reused in the Philippines. The YAKKUM Rehabilitation Centre in Yogyakarta, Indonesia, uses worn tyres to make rubber parts. However, the Centre found that its recycling programme required improvement to enhance the durability of parts and devices made from recycled tyre rubber.

Care should be taken when introducing a new chemical material. Some may require special safety measures in the process of making a device. PVC, for example, emits toxic fumes when burned. If workers are exposed to resin continuously for a full working day, it can cause headaches or loss of consciousness.

H. Imports

Importing assistive devices can be a way for a developing country in the ESCAP region to provide otherwise unavailable devices. As far back as 1950, the international community recognized the need to facilitate the import of assistive devices, in order to support the education of people with visual impairments. Government signatories to the Florence Agreement on the Importation of Educational, Scientific and Cultural Materials, (opened for signature at Lake Success, New York, on 22 November 1950) agreed to allow easy import of braille documents and other articles for use by blind people.

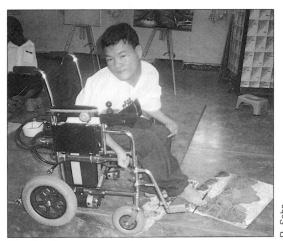

Several countries in the ESCAP region allow import of most assistive devices duty free.

The 1976 Nairobi Protocol to the Agreement extended this, specifying that any articles produced specifically for the "education, employment and social advancement" of people with any disabilities should not be subject to import duties, as long as equivalent articles were not already being manufactured in the importing country.[22]

Since then, countries have generally permitted easy import of assistive devices on condition that they be used by people with disabilities. The ESCAP Secretariat recently conducted a survey with a view to possibly including assistive devices in the Bangkok Agreement on Trade Negotiations among Developing Countries of the ESCAP Region, an agreement to reduce trade barriers and tariffs.

---

[22] See the Mandates Supplement for relevant excerpts from these agreements.

Imports from other developing countries are often more suitable than imports from developed countries, especially when the conditions for which the devices were designed resemble those in the importing countries. Devices imported from developed countries in the absence of local needs assessment and capacity-building have usually had the following disadvantages:

(a) High cost;

(b) Unavailability of spare parts;

(c) Lack of local knowledge for repair and maintenance;

(d) Unsuitability to local physical or cultural conditions.

Prohibitive restrictions on import, such as high tariffs or restrictive legislation, are unlikely to be the best way to deal with these problems. It is more important to ensure that agencies implementing disability policy are aware of these problems and know that expensive, imported high-technology devices are unlikely to be the best choice.

Several countries, including Bangladesh, Bhutan, Cambodia, Pakistan and the Republic of Korea, allow import of most assistive devices duty-free. Others, including India, Sri Lanka and Thailand, allow duty-free import of assistive devices when the devices are imported by people with disabilities or by organizations working on their behalf. Organizing sufficient proof that the devices are imported for bonafide beneficiaries or their organizations can, however, be a long and complicated process.

China produces most of its assistive devices using indigenous resources, but imports a few parts to produce high-technology devices.

Box 14: Imports Related to Assistive Devices

Country	Items imported (devices, parts and raw materials)	Importing from
Bangladesh	Not available	China, India, Norway, Singapore, United Kingdom, United States of America
Bhutan	Wheelchairs, walkers, devices for people with visual disabilities, hearing aids, prosthetic feet, knee joints	Bangladesh, India, United States of America
Cambodia	Polypropylene sheets, aluminium, stainless steel, pelite, ball bearings, cycle wheels, braillers, prosthetic feet	China, Germany, Ireland, Netherlands, United States of America
China	High-technology knee joints, prosthetic feet, polypropylene sheet, core plates in integrated circuits, shin assembly of prostheses	Germany, Japan
Fiji	Wheelchairs, walkers, walking sticks and daily living equipment	Australia, New Zealand
India	Braillers, parts for hearing aids	Germany, Singapore, United States of America
Malaysia	Parts for prostheses and orthoses, wheelchairs, hearing aids, devices for people with visual impairments	China, Japan, Taiwan-Province of China, United Kingdom, United States of America
Maldives	Wheelchairs, tricycles, crutches, walkers, hearing aids, orthoses, prostheses	China, India, Japan, Singapore
Myanmar	Epoxy resin, hardeners, joint bolts and nuts, knee joint, thermoplastics, low-vision aids, teaching aids for blind people, hearing aids, audiometers, batteries	(Information not available)

Country	Items imported (devices, parts and raw materials)	Importing from
Nepal	Tricycles, artificial limbs, devices for blind people, hearing aids, parts for orthoses	Germany, India, Japan, United States of America
Pakistan	Hearing aids, audiological assessment equipment	(Information not available)
Philippines	Knee joints, ankle joints, prosthetic feet, shaft for modular prostheses, upper- extremity prosthesis parts, motorized wheelchairs, hearing aids	Germany, Taiwan-Province of China
Republic of Korea	Prostheses, braces, hearing aids, electronically operated wheelchairs	Germany, Taiwan Province of China, United Kingdom, United States of America
Sri Lanka	Crutches, wheelchairs, calipers	India
Thailand	Myoelectric hands, prosthetic feet, knee-shin parts, plastic polyvinyl acetate (PVA), band saw, benzol peroxide, socket routers and duplicating machine	Germany, United States of America
Viet Nam	Braillers, thermoplastics for artificial limbs, ball bearings for wheelchairs	(Information not available)

Source: Country papers presented to the Technical Workshop on the Indigenous Production and Distribution of Assistive Devices held in Madras, India, in September 1995, and information subsequently provided to the Secretariat. "Not available" refers to information not contained in the relevant papers and not subsequently provided to the Secretariat.

In India, the import of items produced within the country has generally been discouraged. The philosophy has been to encourage the domestic industry and enhance self-reliance. However, in the 1990s, India has begun to liberalize its trade policy and promote foreign investment. This has resulted in the encouragement of imported assistive devices.

In Fiji and Nepal, import duties are compulsory. Nepal charges a one per cent duty on the import of devices by institutions, and a 10 per cent duty on imports by individuals. No duty, however, is levied if the devices are imported for business purposes.

The Philippine Tariff and Customs Code provides no specific exemption for assistive devices. It does, however, stipulate that imported articles of any kind donated to a non-profit organization for free distribution among the poor can be exempted from import duties, if that organization is registered and obtains certification from the Department of Social Services and Development or the Department of Education, Culture and Sports. The devices may not subsequently be sold, bartered, hired or used for other purposes unless duties and taxes are paid. Assistive devices imported for other purposes are subject to tariffs of between 10 and 40 per cent.

Malaysia allows the duty-free import of all devices and their parts, but levies import duty on the polypropylene sheet used for making sockets, as this sheet can be used for other commercial purposes.[23]

Many useful or essential assistive devices are not yet locally produced in developing countries of the region. Since

Increasing availability of devices must be supported by wide acceptance of difference.

each incremental change brought about by an appropriate assistive device helps expand the capacity of people with disabilities to participate in the lives of their communities, reducing duties and simplifying customs clearance procedures will contribute to improving their lives.

Officials in customs departments are often not well informed about people with disabilities and the devices they require for daily living. They are therefore inadequately equipped to make correct decisions. As a matter of policy, government focal points and NGOs working on disability issues should actively seek to inform customs officers through personal contact with them, the distribution of explanatory information materials, and joint seminars.

---

[23] See the Mandates Supplement for examples of the tariff regimes for assistive devices in selected developing countries of the ESCAP region.

CHAPTER VI

DISTRIBUTION

The distribution of many assistive devices differs from the distribution of commodities which can be picked up from the shelf in a local shop. For user-specific devices, production and distribution need to occur in the same place. For example, orthoses can only be properly produced after the user's measurements have been taken and the user has received proper trials and training.

Assistive-device distribution networks need to be established through central Governments, state or provincial Governments, district administration infrastructure, NGOs, public health centres and rural development channels. These networks need to be supported by people who are technically knowledgeable about disability issues. Financial support for such networks will be required to meet the costs of establishment and operation. Without the requisite policy, programme and funding support, such networks will neither emerge nor be sustained.

While the need to supply assistive devices to poor disabled people is widely recognized, success in meeting this need has so far been limited. Many disabled people cannot afford to pay for assistive devices. In such cases, financial support frequently comes from the Government, although many countries have not yet adopted this principle.

In some countries, the number and variety of devices have increased. However, the majority of people with disabilities still do not have them because there has not been a corresponding improvement in coordination and development of the means to distribute the devices, especially in rural areas. Furthermore, many people who could benefit from assistive devices have no information about the availability of the devices or their potential usefulness.

A. Distribution to rural areas

About 70 per cent of people with disabilities in Asian and Pacific developing countries live in rural areas. They commonly face the following difficulties:

(a) Difficulties of access to services and facilities (such as those resulting from difficult terrain);

(b) Lack of infrastructural support (such as the absence of linking roads and public transport);

(c) Lack of understanding among health-care personnel about disability matters, including confused perceptions of people with disabilities as medical cases rather than as citizens or community members with entitlements;

(d) Poverty;

(e) Illiteracy and lack of information about available services;

(f) Absence or inadequacy of statistics about people with disabilities, especially those in rural communities, for proper planning and programme development.

Villages are situated at varying distances from the nearest rehabilitation centres, which are generally located at the level of the province/state, city or district administration. In large countries, the distance a user must travel to reach the nearest centre may vary from a few to a few hundred kilometres. In addition, a period of at least a week is required to make a prosthesis fit and work properly. Long distances are understandably prohibitive for villagers with disabilities. This is because of the cost involved in travel to and lodging at the centre, as well as the loss of income from work opportunities for those who accompany them.

Various local conditions create further difficulties in distribution. Distances may be smaller in mountainous countries like Bhutan and Nepal, but the time involved in travelling from a village to the nearest centre may be longer because of the hilly terrain. Furthermore, landslides can make transportation extremely difficult and sometimes impossible. Countries composed of many islands, including Indonesia, the Maldives, the Philippines and most of the Pacific island countries, may face difficulties in providing adequate means of water or air transportation to enable poor people with disabilities to travel between islands. Monsoon rains make many villages inaccessible for months every year. Even on the mainland, transportation may be adversely affected in the plains by water logging and deteriorated road conditions.

The aforementioned difficulties mean that a country's system of service delivery should have two major features. First, it must be decentralized. A good

Active family involvement is the key step in rural rehabilitation.

transportation and communication system will unquestionably be helpful in distributing devices to local distribution centres. However, with the resources available in most developing countries and the difficulties listed above, it is unlikely that such a system will make centralized production for wide user coverage a realistic possibility.

Second, there should be a large number of local production centres, so that villagers may reach them easily without great expense of time and money. There is currently a tremendous shortage of rehabilitation facilities in rural areas. Many more such centres must be created by Governments, NGOs, and people with disabilities with their families and communities. This effort can be supplemented through rehabilitation camps and mobile clinics.

B. Options for distribution methods and policy

People in Asian and Pacific developing countries have dealt with the above problems in several innovative ways. One approach has been the distribution of disability devices through a camp approach. This approach brings a large number of people with disabilities to a common place (a camp) where they can all receive assistive devices within a short period of time.

Preparatory work for the organization of a camp includes an assessment of needs and the setting of a date for the camp to be organized. Wide publicity is then given.

Camps are usually organized by government agencies and NGOs. The camp approach was first used in India for cataract surgery and immunization, as well as for the prescription and distribution of assistive devices. It is also used in Nepal and Thailand. China has now adopted it for cataract surgery.

Some countries, including Cambodia, extensively conduct mobile workshops. Some NGOs in India have adopted a similar approach, but only in specific and limited areas. A mobile workshop involves a vehicle (such as a van, jeep or boat) which carries within it the necessary tools. The vehicle goes from place to place to provide, repair and maintain devices.

Unlike the camp approach, people with disabilities do not have to travel to reach a mobile workshop. As a result, the mobile-workshop approach is more convenient for people with disabilities and encourages more frequent contact between them and technicians. On the other hand, it involves a greater commitment of resources than the camp approach, especially if production is not decentralized.

Parent groups in rural areas can provide an important means of supporting the distribution of devices. The parents of children with disabilities in villages close to each other can jointly arrange for rehabilitation facilities to be established with the help of an NGO. Many simple devices can be made in a workshop that local people set up at the village level. Such an approach brings down the cost of rehabilitation.

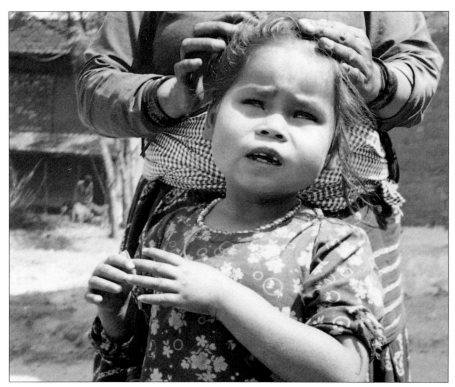

This deaf-blind girl has no access to rehabilitation and assistive devices because the adults around her do not know she can be helped.

Providing services in rural areas for assistive devices alone may not be economical or feasible. Instead, integrated multipurpose workshops can be established in clusters or groups of villages to take care of many of the technical needs of the villagers, including but not limited to their needs for assistive devices. These workshops should include multipurpose technicians with knowledge of mechanical and electrical trades who can perform tasks such as those related to energy generation, hand pumps and tube wells, as well as producing, maintaining and repairing assistive devices. People with disabilities, together with village artisans and mechanics, should have a major role in these workshops.

C. Information dissemination

Many people with disabilities who could benefit from assistive devices do not benefit because of a lack of information. Lack of information is a problem faced not only by people with disabilities themselves, but also by their families, community leaders, health and rehabilitation personnel, and NGOs.

Rural people with disabilities have an inherent disadvantage because most information is generated in cities, in a format directed primarily at the educated urban elite. The problem is complicated by low levels of literacy among many people with disabilities and their families (whether rural or urban). Information in directories, manuals or brochures is of little use to them. As a result, they may lack knowledge of the following:

(a) The existence of assistive devices;

(b) The devices' usefulness for them;

(c) Sources of devices;

(d) Methods by which the devices can be obtained.

There is therefore a need to use existing channels of communication with rural communities to improve their awareness of assistive devices. These channels include:

(a) Radio and television programmes directed at rural communities, including those used for farm broadcasting and agricultural extension work;

(b) The information, education and communication channels of primary health care, community development, rural development, gender equity and child service programmes (government and NGO), which could help disseminate basic information on rehabilitation and assistive devices.

Information of relevance to semi-literate or illiterate villagers must be presented in formats and through channels of relevance to them. Multiple channels may be used to convey the information and reinforce newly-acquired knowledge. Distance learning programmes, folk theatre and poster campaigns are among the channels which could be employed for mutually reinforcing effect.

D. National policies on distribution

The number of government agencies involved in the distribution of assistive devices in Asian and Pacific developing countries varies from country to country. Some Governments fund NGOs or government agencies to distribute and supply assistive devices to users. A large number of agencies could make it easier to reach large numbers of people.

In some developing countries of the region, activities related to the distribution of assistive devices (e.g., registration of users, allocation of funds, follow-up services) are spread among more than one government agency or NGO, with inadequate communication or cooperation among them. This multiplicity of agencies and NGOs and lack of communication may render the process of coordination complex and difficult to manage. It may also result in conflicts in decision-making or implementation. Poor people with disabilities stand to lose the most, as this problem may result in their not receiving the assistive devices they need easily, quickly, and at prices they can afford.

Cambodia relies heavily on NGOs for distribution of assistive devices; all of its workshops are run by NGOs. Government and NGOs work closely with each other. People with disabilities can approach any of the workshops and receive devices free of charge.

There is currently no system of registration in Cambodia, but there is a proposal for starting such a system in the country's newest rehabilitation plan. Local-level government offices for social affairs hold monthly meetings with commune and village leaders in order to inform people with disabilities about the services available. Some centres are equipped with dormitories. Most centres give meals to patients. Many also give them an allowance to cover the cost of transport.

In China, people with disabilities must pay for assistive devices. Different models of devices are available at different prices. This means that poor people with disabilities are often not able to afford the devices they think suit them best. People with disabilities must get their prosthetic and orthotic devices at provincial centres. Each recipient must spend a few days there before receiving a device. Near each such centre there are some arrangements for the accommodation of people with disabilities and their family members, who must meet the costs themselves. China's Ninth Five-Year Plan has introduced a system of loans for rehabilitation to cover these costs.

Distribution of prostheses and orthoses in India involves both governmental and non-governmental systems. People with disabilities or their families can receive assistive devices free of charge, or at a 50 per cent discount, if their monthly income is below specified limits. To receive devices at these concessional rates, a disabled person must have an income certificate to approach a centre which receives Central Government assistance. They are also entitled to some allowances for travel, lodging and food, but these allowances are usually insufficient to cover the full costs. Users usually have to return after a few weeks to obtain their devices. One problem with the Indian system is that there is usually little planning for follow-up sessions. Follow-up is often not even possible because of the lack of trained personnel. There is no registration of those who seek or receive devices.

In Malaysia, people with disabilities must register themselves with the appropriate government agencies. Those registered are entitled to get assistive devices free of charge from centres specified by the Government. They can also obtain the devices free of charge from private workshops, if a device is not available at the specified centres. Furthermore, those registered are paid the cost of board and lodging when they come to the centres to obtain their devices.

The Government of Pakistan provides prostheses and orthoses free of charge to those who apply to the National or Provincial Rehabilitation Centres. It also provides hearing aids free of charge to children, but not to adults.

Sri Lanka provides devices through government agencies and NGOs. The Friend-in-Need Society of Colombo has a programme to provide the Jaipur prostheses to amputees, especially in rural areas. Those who cannot pay for the prostheses can receive them free of charge. Costs are covered by local donations and international aid.

In Thailand, people with disabilities who are registered with the Department of Public Welfare (or its provincial representatives) are entitled to a range of free services, including assistive devices. There are, however, significant difficulties involved in registration.

First, an essential condition for registration in Thailand is the holding of a medical certificate of disability. The Rehabilitation of Disabled Persons Act (1991) does not specify that only government hospitals can issue those certificates. In practice, however, many doctors are reluctant to issue them, even those in government hospitals. Training for doctors to enable them to assess disabilities is not widespread, and does not give doctors the confidence to undertake assessment and certification. The certification form is complicated and difficult to complete. Doctors who have received training for disability assessment generally do not share their training experience with others in their respective hospitals. Those trained are not necessarily the ones who are assigned to assess and certify disability.

Faced with such obstacles, few can obtain the certificates required for registration and free assistive devices. This situation is under review in Thailand, with a view to simplifying the process. However, such obstacles are not unique to Thailand.

The second difficulty involved in registration is that most people with disabilities who need free devices cannot afford the expense involved for transport, board and lodging at provincial capitals where the registration process takes place, although poor people can seek assistance for this.

Diverse agencies are involved in supplying assistive devices in Thailand. The Ministry of Health has principal responsibility for distributing devices, the Department of Public Welfare is responsible for registering people with disabilities, and the Ministry of Education distributes certain devices for schoolchildren. A Rehabilitation Fund, established under the Rehabilitation Act, is available for meeting the costs of repair and spare parts.

In Viet Nam, orthopaedic devices are traditionally the responsibility of the Ministry of Labour, Invalids and Social Affairs (MOLISA). Some units are now being set up under the Ministry of Health Services. Poor people with disabilities and those who acquired disabilities in

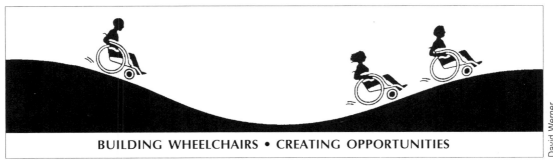

BUILDING WHEELCHAIRS • CREATING OPPORTUNITIES

David Werner

81

war receive their devices free of charge, but others must pay for them. Most users must go to a centre to receive devices. The experience of mobile teams has been unsatisfactory, as there is often inadequate follow-up.

Some countries which face severe economic problems and resource constraints, including the Lao People's Democratic Republic, now ask users to pay for assistive devices which were previously provided free of charge.

CHAPTER VII

REPAIR AND MAINTENANCE

It is a waste of time and resources to provide a person with an assistive device if that device breaks down after a short period of time and cannot be repaired or replaced. Repair and maintenance of assistive devices is a crucial part of any strategy to achieve equality of opportunity for people with disabilities.

The term "repair" refers to modifications made to a device when it is in poor or no working condition, in order to make it work properly again. "Maintenance" refers to the modification or replacement of parts made to prevent possible failures while the device is still working properly, in order to prevent repair from being necessary. Both functions can be performed by users themselves with or without the help of others with mechanical skills. Repair work is more likely to require the help of mechanics or technicians.

The ease of repair and maintenance depends partly on the design of devices, and partly on the availability of infrastructural and technical support near the users. Without some state aid, this support will grow only with time, economic progress and market demand – which may not be primarily defined by the needs of disabled people.

Imported devices are typically the most difficult to maintain and repair, partly for lack of components, but also because manufacturers often do not supply instruction manuals for this purpose. Users may not even know that such documents exist, especially when they purchase the devices. India has faced this problem with respect to braille presses and computerized braille printers.

If people with disabilities and their helpers receive adequate instruction on the maintenance of their devices when they receive them, much less time and effort will have to be spent on repairs. Prolonged exposure to humidity, dust, sand, mud, heat, water and sunlight can cause problems such as corrosion, increased friction in moving

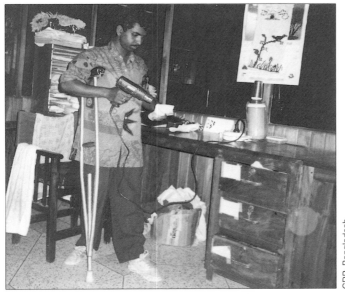

A crutch user repairing an orthosis.

CRP, Bangladesh

parts and hardening of thermoplastics through ultraviolet radiation. Maintenance tips (see the Technical Specifications Supplement) will help users increase the lifespan of their devices and ultimately lower the costs.

A. User acceptance of devices

People with disabilities need a transition period to get used to their assistive devices before they can accept the devices as a part of their lives. This period may vary from a few weeks to a few months, while an individual user decides whether a device is suitable for the way of life she or he wants to lead.

Currently, when a camp approach is used for distributing prostheses in developing countries of the ESCAP region, a second or a third camp for follow-up is usually not held. But follow-up is crucial in the transition period and the period immediately after it, as even a short period in which devices do not function properly may make their users ultimately decide the devices are not worth the trouble.

Many users of hearing aids, for example, stop using them when they have to replace batteries and cords, which are not easily available in rural areas. Similarly, breakage of orthoses among children is usually high. In itself, this may be a good sign, as it indicates that the children have really been using the devices. But if the breakages are not dealt with quickly, children may stop using the orthoses and revert to moving as they did before the orthoses enabled them to become more active.

The use of orthoses requires even more follow-up, with closer attention to detail, than the use of prostheses. An old prosthesis will not work as well as it used to if a child wearing it outgrows it – but an old orthosis, in the same situation, will not work at all.

In one case, a user brought a prosthesis back to the rehabilitation centre after seven years, during which time he had been trying many different methods of repair, as he had had access neither to a repair facility nor to a replacement prosthesis. The result is shown below:

R. Saha

One possible consequence of inadequate follow-up.

B. Cost of repair and maintenance

Cost often deters many people with disabilities from getting their devices repaired or maintained. Many developing countries of the ESCAP region have schemes for providing assistive devices to people with disabilities, or at least those able to obtain the necessary official papers, at concessional rates (see Chapter VI for examples). They do not, however, usually offer a similar subsidy for repairs. As a result, poor people with disabilities find it extremely difficult to afford new parts or new devices. If workshops are far away, the costs of transportation, board and lodging become a further barrier.

Malaysia and Thailand have adopted a policy of subsidizing the cost of repair, replacement and maintenance as well as that of the initial devices. This is helpful, and would be still more so if two more steps were taken to ensure the success of the policy. First, this support must be provided in a manner that is decentralized enough to reach users. Second, people with disabilities need adequate information about where to receive the support.

The cost of repairs is not only monetary. It also involves the time spent repairing devices. In Thailand, repairing hospital wheelchairs has typically taken days or even weeks while technicians wait for spare parts to be delivered. In the meantime, no temporary replacement is available, leaving users immobile for a long period. This results in severe disruption of users' lives. It could be prevented if wheelchairs were loaned to users while they awaited repairs. Loaning of prostheses and orthoses would be inappropriate, but loaning of less user-specific devices would be acceptable, as those devices would only be used for a short period. See Box 8 for a description of an NGO that has attempted this latter solution.

C. Repair and maintenance in rural areas

Repair and maintenance are not, of course, entirely rural problems. Devices like computerized braille embossers, text reading machines, and stair lifts are often difficult to repair even in cities and towns. The reasons can be non-availability of spare parts, lack of local technical skills, or both.

Nevertheless, more emphasis must be placed on the development of repair and maintenance services in rural areas, for reasons outlined above: most people with disabilities in the region live in rural areas; rural areas are deprived of repair and maintenance services because it is more difficult for such services to reach them; and assistive devices are subjected to far more strain in rural than in urban areas.

Local mechanics and artisans can repair some devices, although they may require additional equipment and training (see Chapter VIII for details). Another problem is that mechanic workshops are not always available near users in rural areas. The only alternative this leaves is for users to go to the rehabilitation centre where they obtained the devices, which is a deterrent. Ideally, it would be best to have such a workshop provide the requisite services within a radius of one to two kilometres from each user. While it is often not practical to set up that many new workshops specifically for this purpose, it may be feasible to identify enough existing workshops that, with proper technical inputs, could provide the services required by most assistive-device users.

When local mechanics and artisans are not nearby or are not capable of repairing a particular device, mobile workshops may be of great help (see Chapter VI, Section B, for a description of the mobile-workshop approach). Countries which use the mobile-workshop approach for repair and maintenance include Cambodia, India and Thailand. In Cambodia and India, NGOs provide their services through mobile workshops.

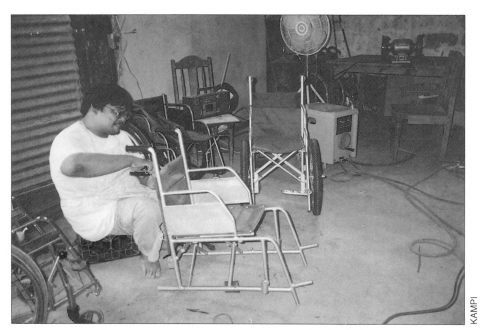

Priority must be given to training person with disabilities in assistive device skills, especially in the rural areas.

Box 15: KAMPI's Wheelchair Projects*

For the past several years, KAMPI and other organizations of disabled people in the Philippines were largely dependent on used appliances, particularly wheelchairs, donated by other countries for use by their members. But these wheelchairs tended not to last because they had not been made to endure the harsh road conditions in the Philippines, especially the rural areas.

There has been increasing interest on the part of governmental agencies and non-government organizations in donating wheelchairs to organizations of disabled persons. Assistive devices from such sources are usually purchased in bulk from commercial establishments; some devices are even imported.

KAMPI's "think-tank" saw the feasibility of raising seed money to start small wheelchair production projects to be undertaken by organizations of disabled persons. The projects would aim both to raise funds for the organizations and to provide people with disabilities a source of livelihood.

In 1995, the *Asahi Shimbun* Welfare Organization of Japan, which has been donating used wheelchairs, contacted KAMPI concerning its interest in contributing expertise to teach KAMPI members the skills of making wheelchairs using local materials.

KAMPI wrote a project proposal to the Department of Social Welfare and Development (DSWD) requesting matching funds for the costs of board and lodging for 12 trainees. The *Asahi Shimbun* Welfare Organization met the expenses of the Japanese trainer and the materials used in the one-week training.

The DSWD provided the matching funds requested and KAMPI selected the participants from organizations of disabled persons who were interested in initiating a wheelchair production project in their respective communities as a follow-up to the training.

Two months after the training was conducted in November 1996, the Association of Disabled Persons of *Iloilo* Province, a KAMPI affiliate, started producing low-cost wheelchairs.

A few months later, the Association of Disabled Persons of Negros Occidental, another KAMPI affiliate, also started to produce its own low-cost wheelchairs.

The wheelchairs of the above-mentioned KAMPI affiliates are made of materials which can be purchased from any local bicycle store. The frames are of steel tubes and the wheels are bicycle wheels. Common repairs can usually be made by a local welder or mechanic.

Compared to the quality of commercial wheelchairs, the KAMPI-produced wheelchairs are sturdier and cost approximately US$135 per unit.

With KAMPI's present limited capital, on average, the output is only 30 units per month.

The national KAMPI office has, however, requested the DSWD to purchase KAMPI wheelchairs when it next makes its annual wheelchair purchase in 1998. As there is still a need to further improve on the quality of the wheelchairs produced, KAMPI will organize another training programme in November 1997, under the auspices of the *Asahi Shimbun* Welfare Organization.

KAMPI plans to start two other projects in this series in the province of *Cagayan* in the northernmost part of *Luzon* and *Cagayan de Oro* City on the island of *Mindanao*. Both projects will be undertaken through a partnership of the local KAMPI chapters and local government units.

Thus far, there are very few women (only three) involved in the wheelchair projects. The workers are nearly all disabled men – deaf and orthopaedically handicapped men are the core workers.

KAMPI hopes to increase the number of women involved in wheelchair production in the future.

---

*   Contributed by Ms. Venus Ilagan, President, National Federation of Disabled Persons, better known as *Katipunan Ng Maykapansanan Sa Pilipinas* Inc. (KAMPI).

CHAPTER VIII

TRAINING

Asian and Pacific developing countries generally lack trained personnel to produce, prescribe, repair and maintain assistive devices. These trained personnel include:

(a)   Orthotic/prosthetic engineers;

(b)   Orthotic/prosthetic technicians;

(c)   Speech pathologists;

(d)   Audiologists;

(e)   Ear mould technicians;

(f)   Optometrists.

The ratio of trained rehabilitation personnel to people with disabilities should ideally be as large as possible. The actual size of this ratio will depend on, *inter alia*, a country's priorities and financial resources. It is likely, however, that it will be difficult in any developing country to train sufficient numbers of rehabilitation specialists to provide needed services.

Instead, it may be easier to provide services in rural areas by training people who are already living in rural communities, especially those who are working there in related fields. Multipurpose technicians, local artisans, and personnel working in various other aspects of rural development can be trained in the repair and maintenance of assistive devices.

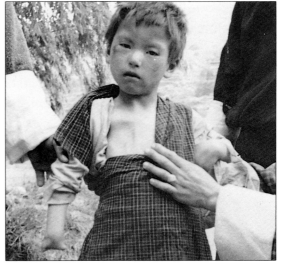

Health care personnel need basic training in disability, to help meet community needs for assistive devices.

For example, many people with disabilities can get mechanical devices, such as wheelchairs and tricycles, repaired by bicycle mechanics, welders and local artisans. These local mechanics and artisans, however, may not have the parts necessary to repair a wheelchair's castor wheel, wheel axle or castor wheel axle. Furthermore, thermoplastics are increasingly used in orthoses, prostheses and wheelchairs, whereas the local mechanics and artisans are usually more skilled in dealing with metal and wood, respectively. Nevertheless, training and equipping local artisans to deal with such matters would be more feasible than attempting to train urban youth as rehabilitation professionals who would be willing to work in rural areas.

In most Asian and Pacific developing countries, people trained as engineers or technicians do not work in the field of rehabilitation. One reason is a simple lack of awareness that engineering and technical skills, especially in mechanical and chemical engineering, are needed and can be effectively applied in rehabilitation. With increasing awareness, more technical personnel may be expected to be involved in addressing rehabilitation issues.

Qualified local orthotic and prosthetic diploma holders in developing countries of the ESCAP region often do not get jobs, especially in cities, where the overall terms of employment could be comparable to those in developed countries. As a result, there is a tendency for this group to migrate to developed countries, where they earn more.

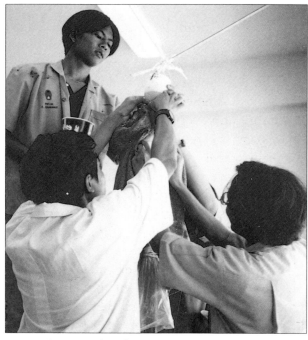

Strengthening local expertise is a prerequisite for sustainability of indigenous production.

Strong policies are required for promoting a more equitable rural-urban distribution of services and personnel trained in assistive devices. These policies will require strong implementation and political determination.

In most Asian and Pacific developing countries, technicians are generally trained on the job, rather than formally. A disadvantage of this approach may be that workers are trained to perform only one aspect of the production of a device. For example, one worker will be trained only in assembly while another will be trained only for metalwork.

Training of local technicians in advanced technical skills helps ensure that NGO projects are sustainable in the long term. For example, most of the workforce in an NGO factory in Phnom Penh is Cambodian, but all the technical experts are expatriates. Local personnel, trained to develop the requisite technical expertise, would free that NGO to use its expertise elsewhere.

A. Recognition of technicians

The Agenda for Action for the Asian and Pacific Decade of Disabled Persons underlines the importance of recognizing rehabilitation technicians, to accord them higher status and encourage them to innovate. Professional technicians should be considered full members of rehabilitation service-delivery programmes, not as mere workers.

Employers of rehabilitation technicians often accord them low status and low wages. In Thailand, assistant technicians do not have job security. In many hospitals, a technician's workshop is not located near the area set aside for rehabilitation. Instead, it is often near the janitor's office and hardware maintenance rooms. This tends to result in poor communication between health professionals and technicians, leading to unrealistic expectations of what the technicians can accomplish. The consequences include poor follow-up. Furthermore, in societies where status and hierarchy are important parameters of functioning, it can inhibit technicians from expressing their views. This can prevent them from helping users in the way they consider most appropriate, and can also stifle the process of innovation.

As well as establishing a system of professional recognition, Governments could distribute newsletters, professional journals and bulletins written by and for technicians. This would not only demonstrate the value of their services, but also help establish a network and a sense of community among technicians to foster exchange of ideas. From there on, it may be possible to develop programmes or other means for technicians to achieve broader knowledge and thus enhance their work on assistive devices.

When new systems of training are introduced, some conflict may arise among technicians. Older technicians may be less well educated and less well trained, but they have higher status because of their seniority. This may make younger technicians afraid of introducing new methods. For this reason, it is important to upgrade the training of older technicians so that they may be technically on par with younger ones.

B. Levels of training

No one group can be responsible for all knowledge and training regarding assistive devices. At least four different groups need to be trained in Asian and Pacific developing countries:

(a) Expert technologists to fulfil multiple responsibilities, including researching, designing and developing new devices, serving as consultants and sources of the latest information on assistive devices, and training others: They could develop and conduct training courses for other personnel, such as mechanics, technicians, artisans and health workers. They could be a useful resource based at, but not confined to, rehabilitation centres in national or provincial/state capitals. Their training programme should follow international practice and guidelines to enable them to make appropriate use of new knowledge produced outside the region.

(b) Technicians capable of taking measurements, as well as producing and repairing devices: They are needed because of the great variety of devices required by people with different disabilities. In rural areas, steps may be taken to train community members as multipurpose technicians who can provide repair and maintenance services for many different types of devices.

(c) Village mechanics and artisans, including blacksmiths and carpenters, who should be trained in the repair and maintenance of devices: The making of many devices requires understanding and study of the human anatomy. These devices should only be produced by those with proper training. The development of training for village mechanics and artisans to support village health workers in rehabilitation is a new area of work to be pursued.

(d) Users, who should receive enough information to be able to make an informed selection of the devices they will be using: In addition, they require training in the safe and effective operation of the devices they select.

C. Training of technologists and technicians

There is a place for institutions which conduct formal training courses for technologists and technicians on assistive devices. Establishing such training courses may be beyond the reach of countries with limited resources, which need to make use of on-the-job training to ensure the production of as many devices as are needed.

Nevertheless, from a long-term regional perspective, training for workshops and production of devices is insufficient. A workforce with the skills for research and development is also needed. One way to develop these skills may be to introduce rehabilitation engineering into the curricula of engineering colleges.

A compact and detailed course over a period of two or three years would be useful to train highly qualified technologists in the area of orthotics and prosthetics. The potential role of such technologists is described above, in Section B on "Levels of Training. (See Box 16 for a suggested syllabus in such a course.)

Course duration for technicians, on the other hand, may range from two weeks to two months and include post-graduate training and technological updates. WHO has suggested the following guidelines for the formal training of technicians:

(a) Laboratory training should include general workshop procedures, woodwork, leather work, metal work, plaster work, thermoplastics, assembly of parts, and assembly of assistive devices;

(b) Academic training should include technology of materials, safety measures in workshop practice, reading of technical drawings, and use of workshop technology.

Proper fitting is essential to ensure that a prosthesis is comfortable. It is therefore important that prosthetic and orthotic technicians be well trained in fitting.

It is important that the training of technologists and technicians be perceived as education, not only as mere training. The tools and techniques in use may be changed regularly. Personnel should therefore be taught general skills and theory, not just the use of particular tools or techniques. They need, in effect, to learn how to learn.

Furthermore, education and training solely in the area of assistive devices are insufficient when not supplemented by education in other areas. Poorly educated technicians may, for example, be unable to understand manuals and other relevant documentation.

In considering the above guidelines, it is also instructive to bear in mind that disabled villagers created and run the Programme of Rehabilitation Organized by Disabled Youth of Western Mexico (PROJIMO). PROJIMO is an outstanding developing country example of an innovative rural rehabilitation programme. The PROJIMO team makes assistive devices and provides rehabilitation services. The skills are acquired mainly through apprenticeship, mutual learning and from volunteer rehabilitation professionals and skilled technicians who devote their short visits to teaching skills. Since its inception in 1981, PROJIMO's assistive devices, designed with and for users, sometimes meet specific needs more effectively than those provided by large urban rehabilitation centres, and at much lower cost.[24]

D. National provisions for training

A few developing countries of the ESCAP region, including China and India, have specific legislative provisions for training rehabilitation professionals. According to 1996 projections,[25] in the next five years, India will need around 1,000 orthotic and prosthetic engineers, 3,200 speech pathologists, audiologists and ear mould technicians, 500 rehabilitation engineers, 2,000 physical or occupational therapists and 50,000 CBR workers. There are several colleges and other institutions that train people in the relevant professional skills. Training is also provided by government agencies and NGOs. The Indian system is geared towards training people in rehabilitation technologies and methods available in India.

China has trained its personnel in orthotics and prosthetics using both internal and external resources. Chinese professionals are sent to Japan on a regular basis, while experts from Japan participate in annual seminars and training activities in China. Recently, under a bilateral technical programe with Germany, China set up the China Training Centre for Orthopaedic Technologists. The Centre will conduct four-year degree courses and enrol 20 new students each year.

---

[24] David Werner, *Nothing About Us without Us*, HealthWrights, Palo Alto, USA, 1998, p. 2.

[25] Indian Association for Special Education and Rehabilitation. *Report on Manpower Development.* Rehabilitation Council of India, Ministry of Welfare, Government of India, New Delhi, 1996.

Box 16: Curriculum for Prosthetic and Orthotic Technologists

The proposed duration of a formal course for prosthetic and orthotic technologists is 18 months and the ratio between laboratory practice and academic subjects 7:1. A model syllabus is suggested here. This syllabus is only a sample, and should be adapted to fit the needs and resources of the country or area in which a course is being established.

Yearly Schedule of Three-Year Course

First Year	Hours
Mathematics	30
Physics	30
Psychology	30
Art	30
Human Development	30
English (Part 1)	60
Physical Education	60
Public Health	15
Introduction to Medicine	15
Anatomy	90
Physiology	105
Functional Anatomy (Part 1)	60
Kinesiology	90
Mechanical Drawing	30
Computer Practice	45
Property of Materials	45
Dynamics of Materials	45
Physics of Prosthetics and Orthotics (Part 1)	30
Introduction to Prosthetics and Orthotics	15
Prosthetic and Orthotic Techniques	105
Biomechanics of Prosthetics and Orthoses (Part 1)	15
Casting and Tracing of Prostheses and Orthoses (Part 1)	60
Fitting of Prostheses & Orthoses (Part I)	60
Clinical Affiliation (Part I)	90
Subtotal	**1,185**

Second Year	Hours
Statistics	30
English (Part 2)	30
Functional Anatomy (Part 2)	75
Clinical Medicine	15
Clinical Neurology	30
Orthopedics	105
Rehabilitation Medicine	60
Clinical Psychology	15
Engineering of Machinery	30
Servomechanics	30
Physics of Prosthetics and Orthotics (Part 2)	45
Biomechanics of Prosthetics and Orthotics (Part 2)	60
Casting and Tracing of Prostheses and Orthoses (Part 2)	195

Fitting of Prostheses & Orthoses (Part 2)	195	Rehabilitation Engineering	30
Professional Management: Prosthetics and Orthotics (Part 1)	30	Biomechanics of Prosthetics and Orthotics (Part 3)	75
Clinical Affiliation (Part 2)	135	Casting and Tracing of Prostheses and Orthoses (Part 3)	210
Subtotal	**1,080**	Fitting of Prostheses & Orthoses (Part 3)	210
		Professional Management Prosthetics and Orthotics (Part 2)	210
Third Year	**Hours**	Related Laws and Regulations	30
Social Welfare	30	Independent Research	30
English (Part 3)	30	Clinical Affiliation (Part 3)	135
Introduction to Pathology	45	**Subtotal**	**1,020**
Functional Anatomy (Part 3)	75		
Physical Therapy and Occupational Therapy	30	**Total**	**3,285**
System Engineering	30		

Source: Excerpted from *The Proposal Plan of Asia Prosthetic and Orthotic Center: Aiming for the Improvement of Prosthetic and Orthotic Services in Developing Asian Countries*, prepared by the Japanese Association for Prosthetics and Orthotics (International Committee), 1993.

In Pakistan, most technicians learn to make assistive devices through apprenticeship with master artisans. There are also formal training courses. The University of Peshawar offers a four-year course leading to a Bachelor's degree in prosthetics and orthotics. All polytechnic and vocational institutions offer courses in carpentry, machinist and metal work. Two universities offer physiotherapy courses.

The Sirindhorn National Medical Rehabilitation Centre in Thailand has a school for training 30 orthotic/prosthetic diploma holders every year. These students come from all over Thailand. In Chiang Mai, a degree course in orthotics

and prosthetics may start within the next few years. A minimum of 12 years of education is generally required for entry to these schools.

Some other countries, including Indonesia and the Philippines, also have schemes to train prosthetic and orthotic professionals. Cambodia has established the National School of Prosthetics and Orthotics, which trains 12 new students per year as prosthetic and orthotic technicians. A school for training in the production and repair of orthopaedic devices is expected to start in Viet Nam in 1997, with the help of a German agency.

The training centres which are being opened have a strong emphasis on the use of thermoplastics, low weight and endoskeletal prosthesis, better comprehension of the alignment of devices, the principles of biomechanics and gait training.

Building on local skills and knowledge to create production and distribution capacity in rural areas is a challenge to NGOs and government agencies concerneed with human resource development, rehabilitation and rural development.

In all these endeavours, it is important to bear in mind that people with disabilities should be given every assistance to participate in the training programmes. If necessary, pre-course education programmes may be organized, to assist prospective trainees with disabilities to attain the basic education level for course participation. Those programmes may include other components designed to encourage the development of self-esteem, interpersonal skills and the ability to make fullest use of a new learning environment. By shifting the focus to include emphasis on the training of people with diverse disabilities in the production, design, repair and maintenance of assistive devices, it may be possible to address in a significant way the need for skills in this field.

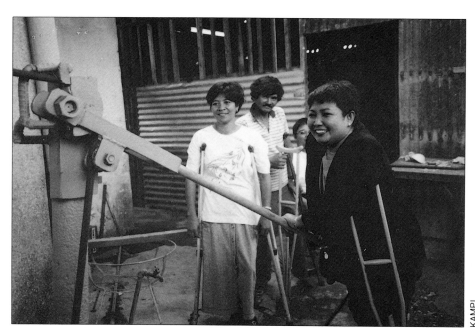

Building on local skills and knowledge to create rural capacity.

CHAPTER IX

INNOVATION, RESEARCH AND DEVELOPMENT

This publication has noted (see Chapter V) that assistive devices imported from developed countries are often unsuitable for people with disabilities living under the physical, social, cultural and economic conditions of Asian and Pacific developing countries. For this reason, local research and development (R&D) and other forms of innovation are of crucial importance for the indigenous production of appropriate devices. This is not to say that developed countries can make no contribution to the development of assistive devices in Asian and Pacific developing countries. On the contrary, it is very important for developing countries to keep up with new knowledge about science, technology, manufacturing and new materials being generated in developed countries, in order to produce local solutions to local problems.

Furthermore, the import of technologies from developed countries has often had the benefit of stimulating local research. Typically, developing countries first adopt an assistive device by copying the design from developed countries (often modifying it just enough to avoid patent restrictions, so that the device can be produced at low cost). Over time, further local-level modifications are made, adapting the device to fit local conditions. This pattern has been observed with regard to the knee joints of AK prostheses, among other devices and components.

Laboratory-based R&D programmes involve considerable investment of funds for equipment, materials, components, energy and specialized expertise. Facilities for testing, making prototypes and field trials are also essential. Expensive laboratory R&D is not, however, the only kind of useful research in the field. Local innovation in the informal sector, often neglected by policy-makers, is central to the development of new devices and new methods of using them.

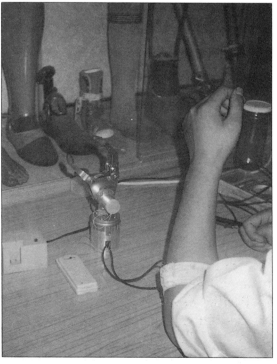

Testing the skeletal myoelectric hand.

In addition, there is a middle level of research which, although conducted in an organized way under an official innovation budget, still does not require the equipment of a full scientific laboratory. Rural technologists and participants in CBR programmes are examples of those who may perform this kind of research. This is distinct from the more spontaneous adaptation to immediate needs that characterizes local innovation.

R&D efforts in the region, whether inside or outside the laboratory, often face the following difficulties:

(a) Poor coordination;

(b) Weak links with users;

(c) Incorrect identification of needs;

(d) Lack of appropriate inputs from specialized personnel;

(e) Lack of funds.

In South Asia and South-East Asia, the growing trend is for countries to undertake their own R&D and to share the information within the subregions. Such trends should be encouraged in other subregions as well as among subregions.

The devices they produce are usually simple, small and effective. There are many examples of such informal innovation, especially in the field of mobility devices and devices for daily living. An example is the making and use, usually in a centre or workshop, of four-wheeled low-height trolleys for tetraplegic people to move about.

Those involved in introducing assistive devices invented in places away from the areas in which they are provided should remember to encourage local innovation as well. While there is a useful role for formal knowledge from outside a community, local people may easily produce an ingenious device that can be adapted for use in other places. Imported technology should be seen as a means of allowing innovation to focus on genuinely new devices. There is no need to reinvent the wheel – or the wheelchair.

The main disadvantage of informal innovation is that, so far, there is lack of a mechanism for its propagation. This means that the innovation might not become as widely used as it could be. Replication could be easier in a small geographical area.

A. Informal innovation

Since rehabilitation centres are rare in villages and remote areas of Asian and Pacific developing countries, people with disabilities in those areas, or their helpers, families or neighbours, have to develop appropriate assistive devices themselves.

B. Participation of people with disabilities

No assistive device should be developed in the absence of consultation with and the participation of people with disabilities, who are the ultimate judges of whether a device is acceptable. Using sophisticated technology to design devices without user involvement may lead to the production of sophisticated devices with no relevance to users' lives and needs.

Knowledgeable people with disabilities who might potentially use the device in question must be consulted from the beginning of the design process. Users should be included directly as members of the decision-making team during the identification of needs, formulation and monitoring of projects, and assessment and evaluation of devices for use. Every device needs to be field-tested among a larger cross-section of potential users before it is produced and marketed.

Users will largely spell out their requirements qualitatively. For example, they may say that a hearing aid has a disturbance. The requirement of reducing the disturbance will have to be translated into quantitative terms by R&D scientists or engineers based on discussions with the users, in addition to the study of available equipment and technical literature. In the long term, it is desirable to train users in the higher-level skills for R&D, science and engineering.

C. Government subsidies and global trade regimes

The role of Government in promoting and supporting R&D is clearly established. This should continue for many more years in the region, especially in developing countries. Governments may have to provide subsidies directly or indirectly to industry and small- or medium-sized entreprises to support their production of assistive devices.

However, the global trade environment after the formation of the World Trade Organization (WTO) may impose some restrictions on the process of providing subsidies for the research, design, development and production of assistive devices. The Agreement on Subsidies and Countervailing Measures in the Uruguay Round, 1994, stipulates that subsidy to R&D will be non-actionable only if the following conditions laid down in the Agreement are met:

(a) Subsidy is non-specific – i.e., not restricted to only a few enterprises, which might include public-sector industries;

(b) Financial support for research, in the case of specific subsidies, is restricted to some percentage of the total project cost.

As only a few industries are likely to engage in the research and production of assistive devices, Government support of those industries could be interpreted as actionable subsidy. If the norms mentioned in the Agreement are not satisfied, any member country of the WTO can raise objections to such a subsidy. This may affect government programmes to support people with disabilities. If the research is of a fundamental nature, it is outside the purview of the Agreement. Developing countries, including India, Indonesia, the Philippines and Sri Lanka, will not be affected for eight years (from January 1995); this is the transition period given to all member developing countries.

D. Patents and intellectual property

The case of the Jaipur prostheses, whose inventors freely transferred the necessary knowledge for production to many countries without receiving royalties, is an exceptional one. A more recent exception is the ground mobility device developed by the National Institute of Design, Ahmedabad, India.

More commonly, assistive devices are patented and their designers receive royalties on their use. A common mistake is the temptation to reinvent technology that is already freely available on a non-profit basis.

Régimes of intellectual property rights are currently becoming stronger and more widely enforced. It is unlikely that assistive devices will be excluded. This presents both advantages and disadvantages for users of assistive devices. The advantage is that patent protection could potentially encourage more innovation and new designs of assistive devices. The disadvantage is that paying royalties will increase the cost of devices.

There is a danger that such cost increases may become prohibitive for buyers (be they users, NGOs or Governments). Some ways of preventing this exist:

(a) Even under wider patent régimes, nothing prevents the inventor of a device from declining some or all royalties on humanitarian grounds, as in the case of the Jaipur prostheses and Ahmedabad ground-mobility device.

(b) Some assistive-device technologies are owned by Governments; these Governments can and should make the technologies available to benefit poor users in their countries and in other countries without charging royalties.

(c) Governments should create guidelines to ensure that sellers of assistive devices do not raise the prices by including the price of a technology which is no longer patented or is not directly related to the device under consideration.

E. Examples of national initiatives

1. China: A national R&D centre

Most R&D in China is carried out by the China Rehabilitation Research Centre (CRRC) in Beijing, as well as various universities around the country. The Governments of China and Japan jointly funded the setting up of the CRRC in 1988, each contributing US$25 million.

The CRRC is, so far, the only one of its kind in a developing country of the ESCAP region. It is dedicated exclusively to rehabilitation research and provides a clear focus to R&D activities in China. It includes a hospital and modern research facilities.

BOX 17:
PROFESSOR JIN DEWEN

R. Saha

In the male-dominated field of assistive devices, it is rare for women to be involved in rehabilitation R&D, especially in the design of state-of-the-art technology. Professor Jin Dewen is an exception. She is the Director of the Rehabilitation Centre in the Department of Precision Instruments and Mechanics at Qinghua University in Beijing. Under her leadership, devices designed at the Centre include myoelectric forearm prostheses, energy-storing prosthetic feet and super-stabilized knee joints. These knee joints help people with disabilities to engage in sports, walk on hilly ground and stand up from a sitting position.

Professor Jin has brought to her profession a high degree of sensitivity to user perspectives. It would benefit users of assistive devices if more such women became active in the research, design and development of assistive devices.

CRRC researchers are currently attempting to develop an intelligent knee joint, with a microprocessor to control the knee movement during the swing phase, as well as wheelchairs capable of climbing stairs. Such wheelchairs may also be useful for rough terrain. Reportedly, however, there is often a lack of funding for the actual production of the devices designed.

Various government factories produce the devices developed at the CRRC. One example is the petrol-fuelled tricycle, which may easily be observed on bicycle paths in China, driven by people with disabilities.

Some universities are also engaged in active research on assistive devices. The Shanghai Tongji University is developing hydraulic knee and hip joints, while the Shanghai Railway University is developing speech synthesizers in Chinese and braille keyboards. The Department of Precision Instruments and Mechanics at Qinghua University in Beijing has developed many devices currently under production, including titanium knee joints for AK prostheses and myoelectric hands.

2. India: A national research project

Indian efforts to promote R&D are broad-based and involve many agencies. One major Government of India initiative was the November 1988 launch of the Science and Technology Project in Mission Mode for the Welfare and Rehabilitation of the Handicapped, implemented primarily by the Ministry of Welfare.

The objective of the Project is to coordinate, fund and direct the development and utilization of suitable, cost-effective devices, as well as methods of education and skill development. The Project uses an interdisciplinary approach. In identifying areas of research, evaluating R&D proposals and monitoring their implementation progress, it involves:

(a) At least seven concerned government ministries, departments and agencies;

(b) Universities and research institutions;

(c) Doctors;

(d) Engineers;

(e) People with disabilities;

(f) Professionals in NGOs.

The government departments involved are the Ministry of Welfare, Department of Science and Technology, Department of Electronics, Planning Commission, Ministry of Health and Family Welfare, Ministry of Human Resource Development and Ministry of Labour.

Full R&D funding is provided to various agencies for project staff, equipment and services. A distinct feature of the Project is the support it provides to the private sector and NGOs, as well as public-sector institutions and programmes.

Areas of research are selected using the following methods:

(a) Constant interaction with users and service providers;

(b) Brainstorming sessions, workshops and seminars with experts;

(c) Identification of laboratory-level technologies;

(d) Evaluation of existing devices;

(e) Study of the scientific and technical literature;

(f) Assessment of available technical expertise;

(g) Bestowing of national awards to the best inventions of assistive devices for their further development.

Interpointing braille writing frames, solar-powered chargers for hearing-aid batteries, feeding aids for children with cerebral palsy, and closed-circuit television with magnification facility for people with low vision are among the devices developed under the Project. They are now produced and provided in large numbers to users. Devices to prevent disabilities have also been developed, such as safety devices to minimize accidents in the use of farm machinery.

Different approaches have been used to transfer knowledge and technology to production and distribution centres and to users. The Government has subsidized production and distribution costs of devices developed in the Science and Technology Project to make them affordable to users.

For further details of this Project, see the India country paper in Part II: Madras Workshop Proceedings.

3. Thailand: Application of science and technology

The Department of Medicine at Chiang Mai University, Thailand, has developed a knee joint and a prosthesis for lower limbs in its workshop. These are now regularly used. The National Electronics and Computer Technology Centre, Ministry of Science and Technology, Bangkok, has started work on the development of an electric wheelchair.

Ratchasuda College, Bangkok, is working on the development of a Thai-language speech synthesizer. A project on developing a communication board for children with cerebral palsy and children with intellectual disabilities has also begun. A Thai-language optical character-recognition package has been successfully developed and is now available in the market. Most of the R&D work is being supported and funded by the Royal Thai Government.

Through technical cooperation, a local innovation in Central Java, Indonesia, can be disseminated far and wide.

CHAPTER X

TECHNICAL COOPERATION

Inter-country technical cooperation is one way to keep the cost of assistive devices low, improve the availability of different types of devices, improve the quality of rehabilitation services, and share solutions to common problems. There are three basic types of technical cooperation: technical cooperation among developing countries (TCDC); technical cooperation between developed and developing countries; and technical cooperation within a country.

Technical cooperation includes such diverse activities as:

(a) Sharing information on the availability of various devices in different countries;

(b) Training technical personnel at various levels;

(c) Sharing technical knowledge with or without royalties;

(d) Performing collaborative R&D in areas of common interest;

(e) Field testing devices developed elsewhere;

(f) Exchanging assistive devices, their components, and their raw materials;

(g) Developing common approaches to quality control;

(h) Sharing facilities for testing;

(i) Convening technical seminars and workshops.

A. Training

Training of personnel is a key area of technical cooperation, as many Asian and Pacific developing countries do not have sufficient numbers of trained personnel for developing, making, maintaining or repairing assistive devices. Moreover, many countries lack personnel with the knowledge to prescribe assistive devices or train people with disabilities in their use.

There are many examples of technical cooperation on training. Technicians from Bangladesh, Bhutan, Indonesia, Maldives, Nepal, Sri Lanka, Thailand and Viet Nam have been trained in India or by Indian personnel over the past decade. Technicians from the Lao People's Democratic Republic and Viet Nam have been trained in Cambodia in the use of polypropylene for lower limb prostheses. Japanese experts visit China and Thailand on a regular basis to train local technical personnel.

Developing countries need funding for their trainees to participate in such training programmes. Development aid agencies have a role to play in funding inter-country training activities on assistive devices, a hitherto little-recognized area of need in human resources development and TCDC programmes.

B. Collaborative research

Collaborative R&D among different countries is a good way to keep low the cost of organized R&D and thus generate new devices more easily. Collaborative research allows scarce skills to be used more effectively.

The cost of research, development, prototyping, field-testing and production of an assistive device is often high. One country alone may have insufficient funds to achieve this. Collaborative programmes reduce the burden on each participating country through a sharing of costs. A successful example of a collaborative programme is the WORTH Trust "Friendship" tricycle. NGOs in India, Netherlands, Sri Lanka and Thailand participated in its design.

To determine the suitability of a device in more than one country, it should be field tested in other countries before finalizing the design. This calls for a joint programme for field testing in the participating countries.

In addition to inter-country collaboration, there is also a need for collaboration and better understanding of the projects taking place within countries. There have been some cases of Governments seeking research conducted in other countries without their being aware that the same research was being carried out locally.

C. Information exchange

Each country must have information related to assistive devices in other countries for technical cooperation to be effective. Currently, few directories of this information are available. There are notable exceptions from Bangladesh,[26] India[27] and the Philippines.[28] A list of producers of assistive devices in this region, with their addresses, is included as a supplement to this document. It should also be possible to use the Internet for exchange of information. The information needed includes:

(a) Types of assistive devices produced;

(b) Names and addresses of producers;

(c) Sources of imports, if any;

(d) Training facilities available;

(e) Names, addresses and areas of specialization of R&D institutions and agencies;

(f) Relevant legislative and policy provisions.

---

[26] Johan Borg, *BREATH: Bangladesh' Resources in Assistive Technology* (Dhaka, InterLife – Bangladesh, 1996).

[27] Research Division, National Society for Equal Opportunities for the Handicapped, *Directory of Indian Assistive Devices: 1995* (New Delhi, National Information Centre on Disability and Rehabilitation, Ministry of Welfare, 1995).

[28] National Council for the Welfare of Disabled Persons, *Catalogue of Assistive Devices for Persons with Orthopedic Disabilities in the Philippines* (Quezon City, Philippines, National Council for the Welfare of Disabled Persons, 1996).

BOX 18: TCDC NEEDS AND INTERESTS

The following table summarizes the interest expressed in TCDC by the countries that responded to the question (see the country papers in Part II: Proceedings of the Technical Workshop on the Indigenous Production and Distribution of Assistive Devices, Madras, India, 5-14 September 1995).

Country	Interested as donor?	Interests as beneficiary
Bangladesh	No	Help in establishing sites for training and production
Bhutan	No	Training and technical or financial assistance
Cambodia	No	Information about available appropriate devices, training
China	Yes: Chinese designs of products, joint ventures, technique exchange	Training and information on distributing devices to the poor and to rural areas
India	Yes: R&D, field testing, technical skill exchange and joint production ventures	R&D, field testing, technical skill exchange and joint production ventures
Malaysia	No	Technology for R&D and production of devices and materials
Maldives	No	Training and personnel for indigenous small-scale production
Myanmar	Yes (unspecified)	Training and production technology, especially for polypropylene
Nepal	No	Training and technical assistance in production, especially of devices for people with hearing impairments
Pakistan	Yes: Training and technical expertise	Unspecified
Philippines	Yes: Technicians skills	Training
Republic of Korea	Yes (unspecified)	Technical assistance for high-technology devices
Thailand	Yes: Low-cost wheelchair production and repair	Development of training for prostheses and orthoses manufacturers and technicians

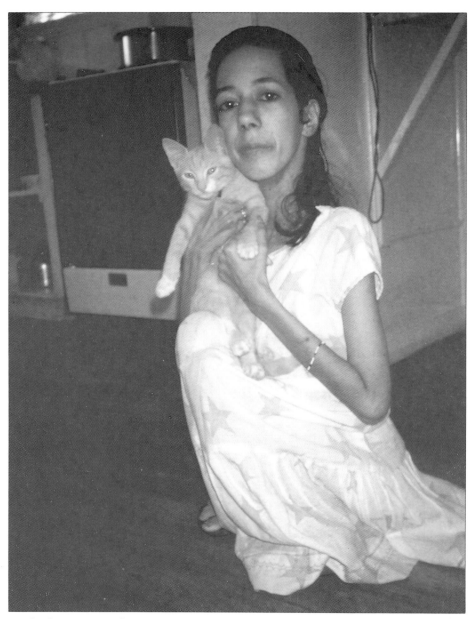

Seek the views of women and girls with disabilities, generate designs to suit their sizes, levels of physical strength and other gender-specific attributes, enable them to participate in a wide variety of activities more easily.

CHAPTER XI

RECOMMENDATIONS

This chapter recommends courses of action for key groups and individuals concerned with assistive devices, based on the information about the region's needs contained in the rest of the publication. Recommendations intended specifically for Governments are contained in the sample national policy and plan. However, those Governments that have an interest in designing, producing and distributing assistive devices will also find this chapter of interest.

A. Device designers

Those creating new indigenous designs of assistive devices, especially those involved in organized R&D, could:

(a) Involve and consult potential users, as well as rehabilitation personnel and local artisans and mechanics, in every stage of the indigenous design process.

(b) Actively seek the views of women and girls with disabilities to generate designs which meet their needs for devices (appropriate to their sizes, levels of physical strength and other gender-specific attributes) that enable them to undertake a wide variety of activities more easily.

(c) Organize national seminars to bring together technicians and specialists (with or without certification) in a forum for technical exchange and to forge a sense of common identity and purpose among those engaged in the field of assistive devices.

(d) Closely follow new developments in assistive devices and related fields, in developed and developing countries, that can be used in indigenous research.

(e) Design mobility devices with sturdy lightweight materials and large bases, which make them more appropriate for indigenous housing patterns and the soil and physical conditions of rural areas in the region, such as sandy surfaces or mountainous terrain.

B. Producers

Those producing assistive devices and device components could:

(a) Adopt a decentralized approach to producing most assistive devices, in order to best meet user needs. Only the least user-specific devices should generally be mass-produced.

(b) Mass-produce components in order to bring down the cost of producing finished assistive devices. This is especially important for components made of new materials (e.g., thermoplastics and titanium), which require high initial investments for special production facilities and must therefore be manufactured in large numbers to minimize costs.

(c) Set up production facilities for new assistive devices through equity participation with companies from other countries that have the technology.

C. Health-care personnel

As they have the responsibility to rehabilitate people with disabilities and prescribe assistive devices, health-care personnel could:

(a) Learn about assistive devices from knowledgeable users and technicians who work on assistive devices, so that they may acquire an understanding of what technical specifications may be most appropriate in a particular case, based on interviews with users and physical examination of measurements.

(b) Acquire an understanding of user lifestyles to facilitate correct decisions on what devices to prescribe (see Box 13 for a sample list of interview questions).

(c) Inform users about the proper use, repair and maintenance of

their own assistive devices when initiating them into the use of prescribed devices.

(d) Prescribe prostheses that are suitable for stumps of irregular shapes and sizes, rather than insisting on standards of amputation that are not feasible in many developing countries.

D. Distributors and repair personnel

Government agencies, NGOs and private-sector agencies involved in distributing, repairing and maintaining assistive devices should:

(a) Extend their services to rural areas away from capitals and their peripheries, since these areas are the most under-served.

(b) Set up workshops and camps to produce and repair assistive devices in rural and remote areas and make it easier for geographically dispersed users to acquire the devices and have access to repair services.

(c) Carefully consider the logistics involved in planning mobile workshops and organize access to adequate facilities, to cover the areas for mobile workshop services.

(d) Organize camps on a continuous basis with good record-keeping and coordination among concerned agencies, in order to provide adequate follow-up services. Funds should be available for the camp-related expenses of the rehabilitation team and its transportation, board and lodging.

(e) Record basic information (names, addresses and types of devices) obtained from recipients of assistive devices, and regularly organize opportunities, either through annual get-togethers or home visits, for consultation with them to follow up on the continuing appropriateness of their devices.

(f) Ensure that information concerning assistive devices reaches women and girls with disabilities in appropriate language and formats, and that services are organized in a gender-sensitive manner to facilitate their equal access.

(g) Pay special attention to the needs of children, as they soon outgrow their assistive devices and need regular follow-up to replace or update the devices.

(h) Ensure that the methods used for distribution of devices (e.g., camps and mobile workshops) are also used to provide repair and maintenance services, with particular attention to appropriate ways of meeting the needs of women and girls with disabilities.

(i) Introduce only those technologies that are appropriate to local cultural, physical, infrastructural and economic conditions and are likely to be sustainable without the presence of technicians from outside the area who may not stay on permanently.

(j) Obtain all instruction, maintenance and repair manuals (and circuit

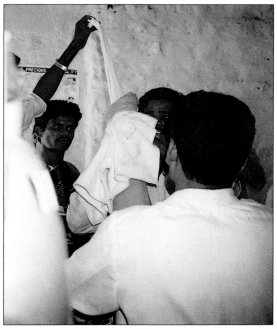

Set up workshops and camps in rural and remote areas.

diagrams, if applicable) for devices that are imported, especially those that have electronic or electromagnetic components, to facilitate local maintenance and repair of the devices.

(k) Ensure that devices provided for use in daily life are indeed designed for daily life, and not for the limited options of a short-term stay in a hospital or similar institution.

(l) Maintain a stock of temporary devices to loan to people with disabilities while their own devices are repaired.

(m) Display every type of assistive device distributed along with the conditions for obtaining them and/or the prices, so that people who need devices can see and select which devices are most suitable to them.

111

E. People with disabilities

People with disabilities and their families, communities and helpers could:

Organize meetings where they can discuss their problems and solutions concerning the use of assistive devices. This would help develop a sense of community among users of assistive devices and facilitate appropriate collective responses to basic problems, especially those faced by all users. It could also encourage new users among other people with disabilities who may previously have been ignorant of, or hesitant to use, assistive devices.

F. Rural development organizations and agencies

NGOs and government agencies active in rural areas but not generally dealing with disability matters could:

(a) Create community awareness about people with disabilities and assistive devices.

(b) Foster community action to enable people with disabilities to participate in community programmes.

(c) Facilitate the formation of self-help groups among people with disabilities.

New challenge for rural NGOs: promoting organizations of people with disabilities.

(d) Start small community workshops to produce assistive devices.

(e) Pay special attention to the production of devices appropriate to local women and girls with disabilities.

G. National governments, and regional and international organizations

National government agencies as well as regional and international organizations should:

(a) Strengthen active regional information exchange concerning assistive devices, by working towards the creation of an information and database, to collect from within and outside the ESCAP region information on technology and techniques, for wide dissemination in the ESCAP region.

(b) Support technical cooperation among developing countries (TCDC) to assist in:

(i) Matching specific needs with available resources and expertise within the ESCAP region;

(ii) Developing means of training more technicians in the indigenous production and distribution of assistive devices, with emphasis on training people with disabilities as well as their family and community members;

(iii) Strengthening the training of engineers and applied scientists to enhance their contributions to indigenous research and design for improved production of low-cost, high-quality and culturally appropriate devices for the poor.

(c) Develop effective approaches to:

(i) Disseminate indigenous knowledge concerning assistive devices, to ensure that semi-literate and illiterate communities have access to assistive devices and related services available within the country;

(ii) Harness community skills, especially among mechanics, craftpersons, health workers, community workers and technicians, for enhancement of local innovation, production, distribution, and follow-up services, including repair and maintenance.

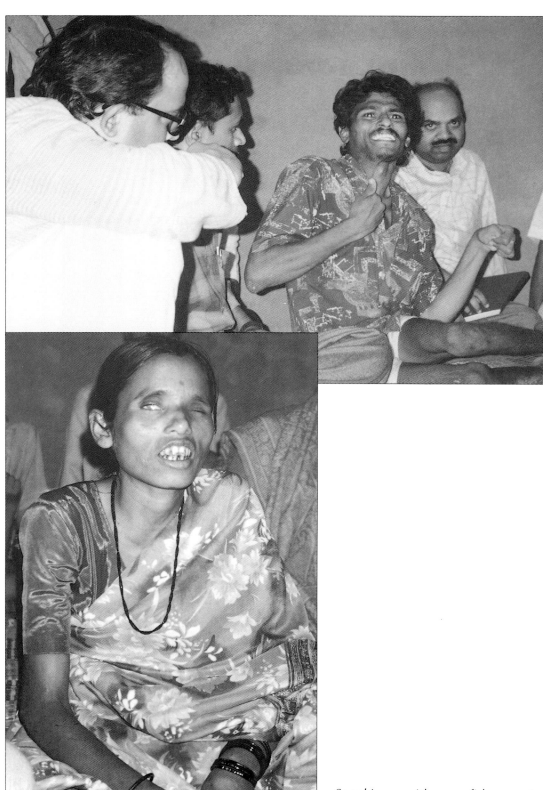

Speaking with confidence in a local association of persons with disabilities.

CHAPTER XII

SAMPLE NATIONAL POLICY AND PLAN

A national policy and plan must reflect firm commitment to disabled persons' full participation and equality.

A. Policy commitment

A national policy and plan for assistive devices should be based on firm commitment to the full participation and equality of people with disabilities in society. That commitment, to be expressed by the highest executive of a Government, should stipulate the goal of the state to enable people with disabilities to participate, as full citizens, in the economic and social life of society,

and the duty of the state to ensure their participation. Government policy statements and programmes at all levels concerning people with disabilities must reflect that commitment.

Towards the fulfilment of that goal, it is essential that the state undertake, *inter alia*, the following:

(a) Train people with disabilities on assistive devices, for informed choice and use as well as the production and distribution of devices.

(b) Make available various appropriate assistive devices that meet the needs of people with disabilities for economic and social participation, supported by the promotion of non-handicapping environments for, and the fostering of positive attitudes towards, people with disabilities.

(c) Allocate adequate funding for promoting the participation of people with disabilities (including through programmes on assistive devices), which, as a proportion of aggregate national and subnational budgets, is at least equivalent to the proportion of people with disabilities in the population.

(d) Require all government agencies with development activities, as well as NGOs, science and technology institutions, academic institutions and organizations of industry that receive

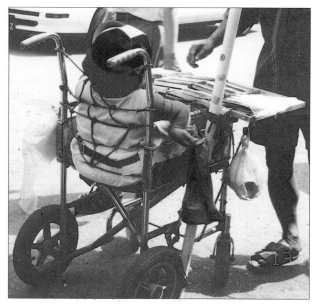

Accord assistive devices a high priority in social policy.

government support, to make budgetary allocations for supporting disability work, including the development and implementation of activities concerning assistive devices which improve the lives of the poor.

(e) Designate a high-level government (or government-recognized) agency, with executive powers and adequate funding, to:

(i) Guide, streamline and monitor the multidisciplinary arrangements of diverse government agencies, NGOs and institutions concerning the production and distribution of assistive devices in ways and at levels which are convenient for people with disabilities, given the lack of accessibility of most infrastructure and services;

(ii) Undertake the necessary measures to facilitate the strengthening of disability data for developing and monitoring action plans on assistive devices at all levels, including promoting the review of all existing survey data sources which could yield relevant disability information and the training of survey enumerators to familiarize them with disability issues;

(iii) Prepare annual reports on the status of work on assistive devices and other aspects crucial to the participation of people with disabilities in society, for dissemination to all concerned parties, including legislative bodies and people with disabilities;

(iv) Undertake the ground work for strengthening legislative and policy provisions to make appropriate devices available to people with disabilities as an entitlement, particularly for skill enhancement, employment, income-generation and community participation purposes.

Within this overall framework, the following are the principles and objectives of a sample national policy, as well as the tasks of international organizations, Governments and NGOs, at national and subnational levels, as contained in a sample national plan on assistive devices.

B. Principles

Government policy on assistive devices may include the following principles:

(a) Recognize that assistive devices are only one aspect of the actions that must be taken to address the problems commonly faced by people with disabilities. Assistive devices must be considered in conjunction with accessible environments, positive changes in social attitudes, and prevention of causes of disabilities.

(b) Accord assistive devices a high priority in social policy as a whole, and include explicit provisions on assistive devices in legislation and policies which affect the well-being of people with disabilities and the availability of services and components for the production and distribution of assistive devices.

(c) Encourage the indigenous production and distribution of assistive devices, including those for people with visual impairments and hearing impairments, as their devices are mainly imported into Asian and Pacific developing countries and do not suffice to meet local needs.

(d) Recognize that the highest level of technology is not always the best. A simple but professional approach is usually the most helpful.

(e) Ensure the development of national capacity through the training of at least four different groups (with emphasis on training women and men with disabilities in all groups):

(i) expert technologists to disseminate the latest information;

(ii) technicians to perform specialized jobs of production, repair and maintenance;

(iii) village artisans and mechanics to make simple devices, and repair and maintain devices in areas where technician services are not easily available;

(iv) users, who should know enough to make an informed selection of devices and be able to maintain them.

(f) Emphasize community-level innovation and support collaboration among people with disabilities, their communities (including local mechanics, technicians and artisans), researchers and rehabilitation personnel.

C. Policy objectives

The policy may have the following objectives:

(a) Encourage distributors of assistive devices, especially NGOs, to locate their services in rural areas.

(b) Develop national capacity in the field of assistive devices, which includes mobile specialists who regularly transfer their experiences from workshop to workshop.

(c) Ensure that assistive devices distributed to people with disabilities are effective, easy to use, inexpensive to maintain, and enable their users to live more active and meaningful lives in their own communities than would otherwise be the case.

(d) Develop a system of decentralized production so that users can have the devices most suited to their needs, with only the least user-specific devices (e.g., hearing aids and braille writing frames) and certain components being mass-produced.

D. International-level actions

Governments and NGOs in the Asia-Pacific region could, in close collaboration with members of the United Nations system, undertake the following:

1. Share resources for training and innovation

(a) Organize inter-country training programmes on assistive devices to remedy the shortage, in many Asian and Pacific developing countries, of trained technical personnel and institutional infrastructure for training.

(b) Promote inter-country collaborative research and development (R&D) on assistive devices in order to optimize the efficient use of the resources allocated to R&D in each participating country.

(c) Promote, and as appropriate arrange for, assistive devices developed in one country to be field-tested in others, in order to contribute to an improvement of design in the long term, and, in the short term, determine their suitability for use in other countries.

2. Exchange information on national and local experiences

(a) Document, for wide dissemination, employment-related examples of modifications to devices, machines and layout of a variety of workplaces.

(b) Use directories of assistive devices as a starting point for promoting intra-regional trade in assistive devices and their components, which may be used directly to prevent production at non-competitive costs. The information may be placed on an Internet website for easy access and include indications of whether producers of assistive devices are ready to export them.

(c) Share experiences (successes and failures) of national programmes related to assistive devices for the benefit of those countries considering such programmes.

3. Facilitate exchange of devices within the region

(a) Facilitate the import and export of assistive devices and their components among developing countries in the ESCAP region through, *inter alia*:

   (i) relaxation or elimination of import regulations and procedures;

   (ii) reduction or elimination of duties on assistive devices, with the aim of supporting intra-regional trade through economies of scale in the production of devices;

   (iii) raising of awareness concerning equalization of opportunities and the role of assistive devices among customs departments and agencies dealing with import and export regulations and procedures.

(b) Produce for publicity purposes information on customs duties and procedures relating to assistive devices, and disseminate the information through the networks of government agencies and NGOs dealing with assistive devices as part of their support for the participation of people with disabilities in development programmes.

(c) Discuss ways of minimizing the negative effect of intellectual property regimes on the cost of transferring technology and knowledge, which would benefit the indigenous producers of assistive devices in the ESCAP region.

(d) Make available those technologies to which Governments own the rights, without charging royalties when the technologies are used in other countries.

(e) Initiate a process of negotiation of some common, appropriate regional quality-control systems acceptable to all developing countries, to facilitate the adoption of quality control by individual developing countries that will not hinder exchange of technologies.

E. National-level actions

Governments at the central level may take the following actions:

1. Coordinate assistive-device services within the country

(a) Foster in-country cooperation and coordination on decisions affecting the availability of assistive devices among all government agencies, NGOs, industry, academic institutions and R&D institutions concerned with assistive devices. The Government agencies include those dealing with social development or welfare, health, education, employment, science and technology, rural and urban development, industry, supplies, finance, commerce and law.

(b) Explore and encourage the use of the following to enhance the production of assistive devices:

(i) expertise in related fields (e.g., science, technology and university affairs);

(ii) new materials (e.g., titanium and its alloys).

2. Provide funding support

(a) Fund directly, and support through other means, the development, production and distribution of assistive devices. This is essential to ensure adequate long-term supply of assistive devices, especially in a developing country.

(b) Cover all costs of, or subsidize, assistive devices for poor people with disabilities, and similarly subsidize the costs of transportation, board and lodging for visits to rehabilitation facilities. Government schemes should permit the provision of more than one assistive device to those people who have such a need in order to pursue training, employment, voluntary work, recreational and/or other activities for meaningful life in the community.

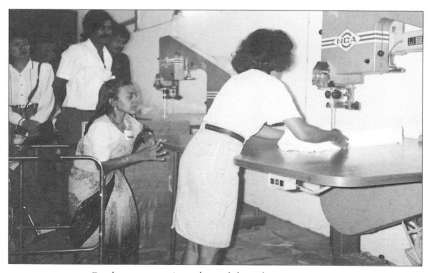

Exchange national and local experiences.

(c) Subsidize the costs of repairing and maintaining any devices obtained under government-supported programmes, and provide financial support to skilled people at the community level for providing these services.

(d) Encourage industries, through incentives with financial benefits, to provide assistive devices and make access improvements to reduce barriers to the employment of people with disabilities, especially in higher-level (management or technical) positions. For example, an industry could be given tax exemption on the purchase of assistive devices, or the Government could supply them to the industry when it employs people with disabilities.

(e) Financially encourage agencies that are or could be involved in disability issues to:

(i) identify user needs in rural communities;

(ii) disseminate information on assistive devices to rural communities;

(iii) set up workshops and camps for producing assistive devices;

(iv) mobilize artisans, technicians and mechanics to work on assistive devices through appropriate training.

3. Adopt appropriate regulations and procedures

(a) Adopt quality-control standards with caution and only when necessary, to avoid discouraging innovation and low-cost production aimed at meeting the needs of the majority of people with disabilities in developing countries of the region.

On-site modifications in industry, adaptations to existing devices, development of new devices – scope for further work to promote inclusion.

(b) Require compliance with standards only for those devices subsidized by government programmes, in order to encourage innovation.

(c) Support the production of adapted motorcycles by eliminating restrictions against the modification of motorcycles and, if possible, providing a subsidy for their adaptation.

(d) Introduce guidelines to discourage sellers of assistive devices from raising their prices through the inclusion of the prices of technologies which are no longer patented, or are not directly related to, the devices under consideration.

(e) Streamline procedures, with maximum consideration to the convenience and limited resources of the poor. This may enable people with disabilities to obtain the devices they need and receive services such as assessment, fitting, training and follow-up, without bureaucratic requirements involving visits to numerous offices on many occasions.

4. Provide and/or support services for training

(a) Use existing training infrastructure for health-care personnel to strengthen training in the production of assistive devices, especially prostheses and orthoses.

(b) Review the curricula for the training of health-care personnel, in order to include training on rehabilitation and assistive devices.

(c) Establish a system of recognizing rehabilitation technicians in order to confer higher status on them in the societies of the Asian and Pacific developing countries.

(d) Develop expertise in the design and production of dies for thermoplastic components, as their use will likely increase with the increasing use of thermoplastics in assistive devices.

(e) Introduce rehabilitation engineering into the curriculum of engineering colleges and universities, especially those that are government-supported.

(f) Promote the inclusion of people with disabilities in training programmes on assistive devices, in the following respects:

(i) as participants, to be trained in various aspects of the production and distribution of assistive devices;

(ii) as resource persons, to advise on the substantive content of the training programme and/or to teach, particularly on user perspectives concerning design, production, assessment, fitting and the usefulness of devices for the empowerment of people with disabilities.

(g) Upgrade the training of older technicians to put them on par with younger ones when new training methods and techniques are introduced.

F. Subnational-level actions

Governments at local, municipal, regional, provincial or state levels may take the following actions:

1. Collect data on people with disabilities and assistive devices

(a) Include in surveys (e.g., those on households, poverty alleviation, employment, education and health), questions to seek data on people with disabilities and introduce measures to estimate data on diverse groups with disabilities, the extent of their representation among the poor and unemployed, and their levels of literacy, as well as on other indicators. Planning concerning the production and distribution of assistive devices and training for these functions requires such data. General data are required to monitor whether existing demand is being met.

(b) Support, in appropriate ways, the introduction of training for survey teams on the formulation of questions to seek information on disabilities, enumeration, data analysis and the use of data from a variety of existing sources, to enhance the quality of data which can be used for the development of a national policy plan and programme on assistive devices.

(c) Introduce measures for the regular identification of local sources for the production of components, to facilitate the increased local production, availability and price competitiveness of components. Producers may then obtain parts directly rather than attempting to produce them at non-competitive costs.

(d) Identify types of jobs in the production and distribution of assistive devices which can be efficiently carried out by people with disabilities, both in the organized and informal sectors, and make that information available to all parties in a position to support the training and employment of people with disabilities for the jobs identified.

(e) Interview local people with disabilities to seek information on informal innovations of devices produced locally, and support their sharing that information with people with disabilities within and outside of the country, or at subregional or regional levels.

(f) Compile and update (e.g., through postal questionnaire surveys via government and NGO channels) a directory of all locally available devices with names and addresses of producers and distributors. Include the market prices of the devices and their basic features in the directory. Pay special attention to the inclusion in the directory of new, small and innovative producers and distributors, and to those producing devices for women and girls with disabilities.

2. Publicize and distribute information about assistive devices

(a) Provide basic knowledge about assistive devices, and their liberating potential for people with disabilities, to all officials engaged in implementing rural and urban development programmes, especially those for poverty alleviation and infrastructure development.

(b) Develop and implement training programmes for village artisans and mechanics on strengthening their skills to repair and maintain assistive devices and innovate new designs.

(c) Publicize information on assistive devices through government agencies (including primary health-care centres), NGOs, civic groups (including those not working on disability matters), institutions of higher learning, R&D institutions, distance learning programmes, industry associations, users, their families and helpers, and the mass media (especially programmes directed at rural communities).

(d) Use fairs and other local events to create awareness about the availability of the devices. The information must be placed where people, especially in rural areas, have easy access to it. Make information on assistive devices available on an Internet website, wherever facilities exist, and encourage users of the website to offer new information through e-mail as well.

(e) Develop appropriate ways of explaining the design and production of assistive devices to members of local communities with limited exposure to sophisticated technology, in order to encourage them to work on assistive devices.

(f) Facilitate meetings of users of assistive devices in small geographical areas, to:

   (i) enable them to share problems and solutions in the use of assistive devices;

   (ii) help them encourage other people with disabilities to learn about assistive devices and overcome hesitation about using them;

   (iii) support the development of a collective voice of people with disabilities on local issues concerning assistive devices, and approach local development resources on resolving these issues.

(g) Publicize the results of surveys which include questions on disability data (see Section F 1. of this Chapter) and ensure their dissemination to agencies working with local communities, especially those in the places where the surveys have been conducted.

(h) Convene meetings of device distributors to discuss local information with them. This would facilitate the planning of distribution services.

3. Provide or support services for the production, distribution, repair and maintenance of devices

(a) Equip, with facilities and trained personnel to prescribe and produce assistive devices, all hospitals located in parts of the country without rehabilitation centres.

(b) Establish, with village community participation (e.g., contribution of land and services for building and management), integrated multipurpose workshops to address the technical needs of villages, including those related to assistive devices, where such workshops do not already exist. Government funding for the integrated multipurpose workshops could be provided for a minimum of five to seven years.

(c) Develop monitoring mechanisms to ensure that the production and distribution of assistive devices meet the needs of all people with disabilities, especially those in poor communities.

(d) Support the formation of local groups, composed of users of assistive devices and their family members. NGOs, policy makers, and professionals, including technologists, may be encouraged to support the groups through the provision of resource allocations and technical advice, as required. These groups may pursue local actions to ensure the quality and coverage of services concerning assistive devices for local-community users, with special attention to children, and women and girls with disabilities.

(e) Encourage those organizations and agencies which are active in rural areas but not working on disability matters to assist in the provision of basic rehabilitation services, including assistive devices, through financial and other support measures. See Section F of Chapter XI for sample measures that the organizations and agencies may take.

(f) Introduce and strengthen the inclusion of rehabilitation and assistive-device services in programmes for primary health care, child development, youth skills development and other aspects of community development.

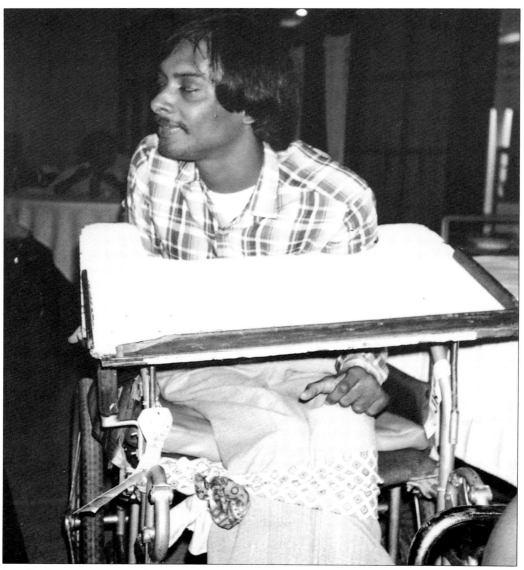

Madhab, peer counsellor at the Centre for the Rehabilitation of the Paralysed, Savar, Bangladesh.

GLOSSARY

alignment: The degree to which the parts of a prosthesis or orthosis fit into the correct position with the user's body and with one another.

assistive device: An item that can directly enable people with disabilities to participate in activities of daily life.

brace: See orthosis.

caliper: See orthosis.

disability: Any restriction or lack (resulting from an impairment) of ability to perform an activity in the manner or within the range considered normal for a human being.

endoskeletal prosthesis: A lower-limb prosthesis whose strength comes from a central tube, or pylon, on the inside of it. The shape and appearance of the prosthesis are provided by a covering, usually made of foam or polypropylene.

exoskeletal prosthesis: A prosthesis in which the shank is shaped like a leg and forms the outside of the prosthesis.

foot-drop: The condition that causes a foot to drop downward so that only the toes touch the ground when the foot is lifted. It results from the effect of gravity on a weak ankle.

gait: Pattern of walking.

handicap: The disadvantage for a given individual, resulting from an impairment or a disability, that limits or prevents the fulfilment of a role that is normal (depending on age, sex, and social and cultural factors) for that individual.

impairment: Any loss or abnormality of psychological, physiological or anatomical structure or function.

keel: A solid piece, located in the central part of a prosthetic foot, around which the whole foot is moulded.

locomotor disability: A disability that affects movement of body parts.

modular: Made of a number of smaller, units (modules) which can be assembled in a workshop to make a complete device. Each module is interchangeable with other modules having the same or similar function.

myoelectric hand: An artificial hand which uses electrodes to pick up muscle contractions in the stump, using these for movement.

127

orthosis: A device fitted to an existing limb to keep that limb in a functional position. Orthoses are also called braces or calipers. Small orthoses, especially for upper extremities, are also called splints.

prosthesis: A device which replaces a missing body part to restore its function and appearance, such as an artificial limb.

pylon: See endoskeletal prosthesis.

shank: The structural member that connects the foot-ankle assembly of a lower-limb prosthesis to the socket or the knee unit. The primary purpose of a shank is to transfer the load of body weight to the foot and the ground surface.

socket: The portion of an artificial limb which comes in contact with a stump. It is shaped to hold the stump.

splint: See orthosis.

stump: The remaining portion of an amputated limb, which comes into contact with an artificial limb.

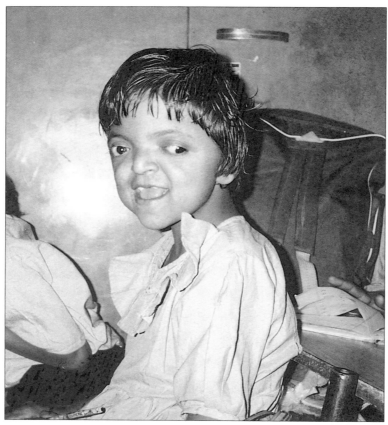

Every child's right to education is often overlooked in the case of children with disabilities.

LIST OF ABBREVIATIONS

AFO	ankle foot orthosis	**ICRC**	International Committee of the Red Cross
AK	above-knee	**ISO**	International Standards Organization
ALIMCO	Artificial Limb Manufacturing Company (India)	**KAFO**	knee ankle foot orthosis
APHT	Association of the Physically Handicapped of Thailand	**KAMPI**	Katipunan Ng Maykapansanan Sa Pilipinas Inc. (National Federation of Disabled Persons, Philippines)
BK	below-knee		
CBR	community-based rehabilitation		
CP	cerebral palsy	**MSALVA**	Ministry of Social Affairs, Labor and Veterans Affairs (Cambodia)
CRP	Centre for the Rehabilitation of the Paralysed (Bangladesh)		
CRRC	China Rehabilitation Research Centre	**NGO**	non-governmental organization
DST	Department of Science and Technology (India)	**NRC**	National Rehabilitation Centre for the Physically Handicapped (Indonesia)
ESCAP	Economic and Social Commission for Asia and the Pacific		
		POP	plaster of Paris
FESPIC	Far East and South Pacific Games for Disabled Persons	**PTB**	patellar-tendon-bearing
		PVC	polyvinyl chloride
FRO	floor reaction orthosis	**R&D**	research and development
HI	Handicap International	**SACH**	solid ankle cushion heel
HDPE	high-density polyethylene		
HKAFO	hip knee ankle foot orthosis	**SCI**	spinal-cord injury
HRD	Human resources development	**TCDC**	technical cooperation among developing countries
HRDC	Hospital and Rehabilitation Centre for Disabled Children (Nepal)	**WHO**	World Health Organization
		WTO	World Trade Organization

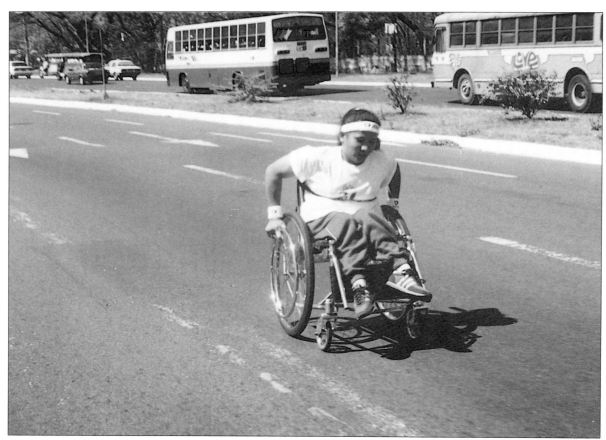

Gender equality in the disability movement – and in access to appropriate devices.

KAMPI

MEMBERS AND ASSOCIATE MEMBERS OF ESCAP

Members (51)

1. Afghanistan
2. Armenia
3. Australia
4. Azerbaijan
5. Bangladesh
6. Bhutan
7. Brunei Darussalam
8. Cambodia
9. China
10. Democratic People's Republic of Korea
11. Fiji
12. France
13. India
14. Indonesia
15. Islamic Republic of Iran
16. Japan
17. Kazakhstan
18. Kiribati
19. Kyrgyzstan
20. Lao People's Democratic Republic
21. Malaysia
22. Maldives
23. Marshall Islands
24. Micronesia (Federated States of)
25. Mongolia
26. Myanmar
27. Nauru
28. Nepal
29. Netherlands
30. New Caledonia
31. Pakistan
32. Palau
33. Papua New Guinea
34. Philippines
35. Republic of Korea
36. Russian Federation
37. Samoa
38. Singapore
39. Solomon Islands
40. Sri Lanka
41. Tajikistan
42. Thailand
43. Tonga
44. Turkey
45. Turkmenistan
46. Tuvalu
47. United Kingdom of Great Britain and Northern Ireland
48. United States of America
49. Uzbekistan
50. Vanuatu
51. Viet Nam

Associate Members (9)

1. American Samoa
2. Cook Islands
3. French Polynesia
4. Guam
5. Hong Kong, China
6. Macau
7. New Caledonia
8. Niue
9. Northern Mariana Islands

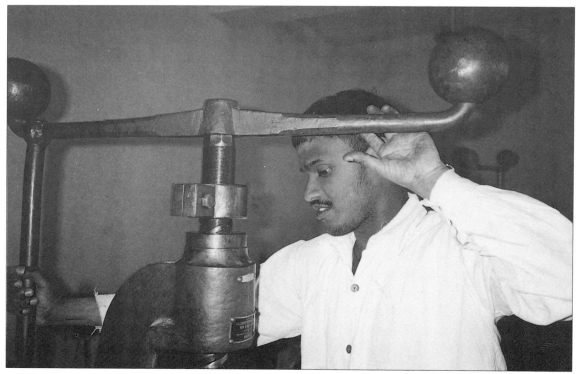

Blind persons can learn engineering trades, given the right tools and proper guidance.

SELECTED REFERENCES

Australian Council for Rehabilitation of Disabled and International Commission on Technical Aids, Building and Transportation (ICTA)[1] Information Centre. *Asia Pacific disability aids and appliances handbook.* Curtin, A.C.T., Australia, 1982.

Appropriate Health Resources and Technologies Action Group (AHRTAG). *Essential CBR information resources: an international listing of publications.* London, 1996.

Borg, Johan. *BREATH: Bangladesh's resources in assistive technology.* Dhaka, Bangladesh, InterLife, 1996.

European Commission. *Userfit: a practical guide handbook on user-centred design for assistive technology.* Brussels-Luxembourg, ECSC-EC-EAEC, 1996.

Handicap International Technical Publishing Department. *A plastic caliper for children: a technique of appliance and physical therapy for polio affected children.* Training Centre, Pondicherry, India, second quarter, 1994. ISBN: 2-909064-14-X.

Helander, Einer and others. *Training in the community for people with disabilities.* Geneva, World Health Organisation (WHO), 1989. Published also in French, Portuguese and Spanish.

Ho Nhu Hai, "Motor Disabled People in Rural Areas of Vietnam", *Round Table Meeting on the Integration of Disabled People in Agricultural and Agro-Industry Systems organised by the Food and Agriculture Organisation of the United Nations, 13-15 May, Bangkok, Thailand, 1997.*

Hotchkiss, Ralf. *Independence through mobility: a guide to the manufacture of the ATI-*

Hotchkiss wheelchair. Washington, D.C., Appropriate Technology International, 1985.

Human Resources Department Canada. *Tips, tools and techniques: homes maintenance and hobbycraft, people with disabilities and seniors.* Ottawa, 1995.

ICTA Information Centre. *The disabled person as a consumer of technical aids.* Bromma, Sweden, December 1984.

ICTA Information Centre and African Medical and Research Foundation. *Local Production of Appropriate Technical Aids for Disabled People: Report from RI Post-Congress Workshop in Kibwezi, Kenya, 14-16 September, 1992.* Order no. 94528. ISBN 91-88336-23-9.

---

[1] ICTA now stands for International Commission on Technology and Accessibility.

ICTA Information Centre and AHRTAG. *Appropriate Technical Aids for DisabledPeople: Ways and Means for Their Production in the Third World. Report from a seminar in Bombay, India, September 22-26, 1986.* ISBN no. 91-8631-027-5.

ICTA Information Centre, Rehabilitation International. *Report from the ICTA seminar on Appropriate Technology – An Essential Part of a CBR programme, 12 September, 1995, Jakarta, Indonesia.* Vallingby, Sweden, Order no. 96530, ISBN 91-88336-74-3.

India. Ministry of Welfare. Rehabilitation Council of India. Indian Association for Special Education and Rehabilitation. *Report on manpower development.* New Delhi, January 1996.

_____ Rehabilitation Technology Centre. DRC Scheme. *Aids and appliances: a report on availability and research and development activities.* New Delhi, February 1990.

_____ Rehabilitation Technology Centre. *Research and development activities for development of assistive devices for people with disabilities.* New Delhi, 1995.

_____ Research Division. National Society for Equal Opportunities for the Handicapped. National Information Centre on Disability and Rehabilitation. *Directory of Indian Assistive Devices: 1995.* New Delhi, 1995.

ISPO. *Report of the Consensus Conference on Appropriate Prosthetic Technology for Developing Countries, Phnom Penh, Cambodia, 5-10 June, 1995.*

Lagerwall, Tomas. *Appropriate Aids and Equipment for Disabled People in Africa: Ways and Means for Local Production in the Third World : Report from a seminar in Harare, Zimbabwe, 20-26 March, 1988.* Bromma, Sweden, ICTA. ISBN: 91-86310-53-4.

Mathu, M.K. *The Jaipur above-knee prosthetic systems: fabrication manual.* Jaipur, India, SMS Medical Centre, 1989.

Minto, Hasan, and Awan, Haroon. *Management of low vision for developing countries.* Rawalpindi, Pakistan, Al-Shifa Eye Hospital and Pakistan Institute of Ophthalmology, 1995.

Olney, S. and others. *Rehabilitation technology in community based rehabilitation: a compendium.* Kingston, Ontario, Canada, International Centre for the Advancement of Community Based Rehabilitation (ICACBR), September 1995.

Philippines. National Council for the Welfare of Disabled Persons. *Guidebook on assisting disabled and elderly people who travel.* Quezon City, Philippines, 1995.

_____ Technical Cooperation Centre (TCC). *Catalogue of assistive devices for persons with orthopaedic disabilities in the Philippines.* Quezon City, Philippines, 1996.

Saha, R. Role of technology in rehabilitation of handicapped. *Standards India.* (New Delhi) v. 6, January 1993.

Saha R. and others. Study of wheelchair operations in rural areas covered under the District Rehabilitation Centre (DRC) scheme. *Indian journal of disability and rehabilitation* (New Delhi), July-December 1990.

_____ Technology and employment opportunities for disabled in industry. *Indian journal of disability and rehabilitation* (New Delhi), January-June 1992.

_____ Uncleared landmines: the scope of the problem in Africa, Asia, the Middle East, the Americas and Europe. *UNIDIR Newsletter* No. 28/29:47, December 1994/May 1995.

Spastics Society of India. *UPKRAN: a manual of aids for the multiply handicapped.* Bombay, India.

United Nations. Economic and Social Commission for Asia and the Pacific. *Promotion of non-handicapping physical environments for disabled persons: guidelines.* (ST/ESCAP/1492).

_____ European Commission for Europe, in cooperation with International Federation for Medical and Biological Engineering. *Rehabilitation Engineering: review publication prepared for the World Summit for Social Development.* Geneva and New York, 1995. United Nations publication, Sales No. E 94.II.E.17. ISBN 92-1-116595-4. (ECE/ENG.Aut/55)

_____ United Nations Childrens' Fund. *Relief and rehabilitation of traumatized children in war situations.* Paper submitted for the World Summit on Children, 1990.

_____ United Nations Development Programme. *Prejudice and dignity: an introduction to community-based rehabilitation* by Einer Helander. 1993. United Nations publication, Sales No. E93-III-B.3.

Werner, David. *Disabled village children: a guide for community health workers, rehabilitation workers and families.* Palo Alto, California, Hesperian Foundation, 1988.

_____ *Helping health workers learn.* Palo Alto, California, HealthWrights, 1982.

_____ *Nothing about us without us: developing innovative technologies for, by and with disabled persons.* Palo Alto, California, HealthWrights, 1998.

_____ and Sanders, David. *Questioning the solution: the politics of primary health care and child survival.* Palo Alto, California, HealthWrights, 1997.

WHO. *Guidelines for training personnel in developing countries for prosthetic and orthotic services.* (Based on the outcome of a WHO consultation on the training of personnel for prosthetic and orthotic services in developing countries, WHO Eastern Mediterranean Regional Office, Alexandria, Egypt, June 1990.

_____ *Guidelines for the prevention of deformities in polio.* Geneva, 1995.

_____ *Promoting the development of young children with cerebral palsy: a guide for mid-level rehabilitation.* Geneva, 1993.

SELECTED REFERENCES

全国残疾人用品开发供应总站
General Services in Developing & Supplying
Aids for the Disabled

1995

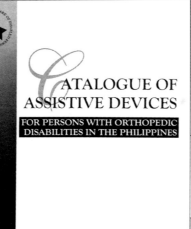

CATALOGUE OF
ASSISTIVE DEVICES
**FOR PERSONS WITH ORTHOPEDIC
DISABILITIES IN THE PHILIPPINES**

Prepared by the TECHNICAL COOPERATION CENTER (TCC)

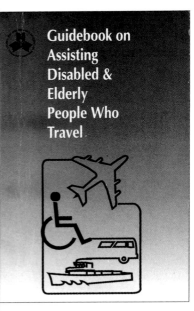
Guidebook on
Assisting
Disabled &
Elderly
People Who
Travel

HANDBOOK ON
PAPER-BASED
TECHNOLOGY

*How To Make Assistive Devices,
Home Decors, Furnitures and
Novelty Items out of Used Papers*

NATIONAL
COUNCIL FOR
THE WELFARE
OF DISABLED
PERSONS

ASIA – PACIFIC
DISABILITY AIDS AND APPLIANCES HANDBOOK

PART 1 : MOBILITY AIDS   december 1982

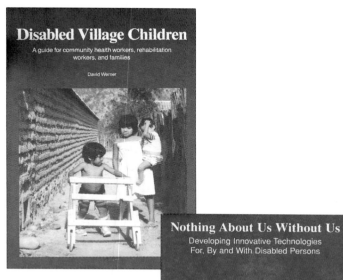

Disabled Village Children

A guide for community health workers, rehabilitation workers, and families

David Werner

BREATH

Bangladesh' Resources in Assistive Technology

InterLife - Bangladesh
P.O. Box 5140
New Market
Dhaka - 1205

Author:
Johan Borg

March 1996

Nothing About Us Without Us

Developing Innovative Technologies
For, By and With Disabled Persons

by David Werner
author of Disabled Village Children
and Where There Is No Doctor

RESEARCH AND DEVELOPMENT ACTIVITIES
FOR DEVELOPMENT OF
ASSISTIVE DEVICES FOR PEOPLE
WITH DISABILITIES

REHABILITATION TECHNOLOGY CENTRE
MINISTRY OF WELFARE
GOVERNMENT OF INDIA
1995

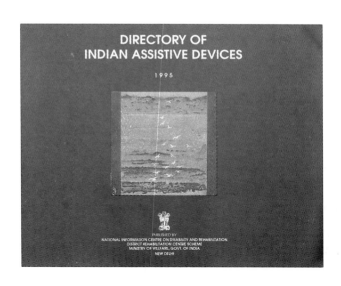

DIRECTORY OF INDIAN ASSISTIVE DEVICES

1995

PUBLISHED BY
NATIONAL INFORMATION CENTRE ON DISABILITY AND REHABILITATION
DISTRICT REHABILITATION CENTRE SCHEME
MINISTRY OF WELFARE, GOVT. OF INDIA
NEW DELHI

Photo Credit

Credit Due	Page Number
John Ang, Department of Social Work and Psychology, National University of Singapore	47
Association of People with Disability (ADP), Bangalore, India	22
Centre for the Rehabilitation of the Paralysed (CRP), Savar, Bangladesh	24, 28, 36 (top), 37, 38, 41, 42, 44 (bottom), 83
Handicap International – Thailand	vi, xiv
KAMPI	86, 96, 115, 130
Topong Kulkhanchit, Association of the Physically Handicapped , Thailand (APHT)	27, 45, 49
Ministry of Welfare, Government of India	2, inside back cover
Rehabilitation Technology Centre, Ministry of Welfare, Government of India	54
R. Saha, Department of Science and Technology. Government of India	18 (top), 26, 30, 48 (top), 56, 71, 84, 97, 101
Antony Samy, WORTH Trust, Katpadi, India	53 (top)
San Yuenwah, Social Development Division, ESCAP	11, 13, 14, 15, 16, 17, 18 (bottom), 19, 21, 29, 31, 32, 48 (bottom) 50, 51 (if you find photo), 52, 53 (bottom) 57, 58, 60, 65, 69, 74, 76, 78, 89, 90, 103, 104, 108, 111, 112, 114, 116, 120, 121, 126, 128, 132
Cyril Siriwardene, Sri Lanka Foundation for the Rehabilitation of the Disabled	1, 23
D.S. Vohra, Nevedac Prosthetic Centre, Chandigarh, India	34, 39, 40
Wang Tao, China Disabled Persons' Federation (CDPF)	62
David Werner, HealthWrights, Palo Alto, USA	44 (top)
Yakkum Rehabilitation Centre, Yogyakarta, Indonesia	36 (bottom)

Illustration Credit

Credit Due	Page Number
Siriwalla Kosin, Population Division, ESCAP	13
National Institute of Design, Ahmedabad, India	43
David Werner, HealthWrights, Palo Alto, USA	9, 54, 81, 82